Being Twice Exceptional

of related interest

An Adult with an Autism Diagnosis
A Guide for the Newly Diagnosed
Gillan Drew
ISBN 978 1 78592 246 6
eISBN 978 1 78450 530 1

Our Autistic Lives
Personal Accounts from Autistic Adults Around the World Aged 20 to 70+
Edited by Alex Ratcliffe
ISBN 978 1 78592 560 3
eISBN 978 1 78450 953 8

Defining Autism
A Guide to Brain, Biology, and Behavior
Emily L. Casanova and Manuel F. Casanova
ISBN 978 1 78592 722 5
eISBN 978 1 78450 349 9

Being Twice Exceptional

Melanie Hayes

Jessica Kingsley Publishers
London and Philadelphia

First published in Great Britain in 2022 by Jessica Kingsley Publishers
An imprint of Hodder & Stoughton Ltd
An Hachette Company

1

A CIP catalogue record for this title is available from the
British Library and the Library of Congress

ISBN 978 1 78775 962 6
eISBN 978 1 78775 963 3

Printed and bound in the United States by Integrated Books International

Jessica Kingsley Publishers' policy is to use papers that are natural,
renewable and recyclable products and made from wood grown in
sustainable forests. The logging and manufacturing processes are expected
to conform to the environmental regulations of the country of origin.

Jessica Kingsley Publishers
Carmelite House
50 Victoria Embankment
London EC4Y 0DZ

www.jkp.com

Contents

Part 1: Autism, Giftedness, and Potential

Autistic and Gifted 9

Labels Don't Define Me 15

Learning Firsthand 20

Powerful Words 27

Being an Advocate 34

Part 2: Stories

2eA Grows Up 41

Asynchronous at College 61

Making It Work at Work 81

Homekeeping 101

Personal Care 120

Having Fun 133

Dating and Sex 148

Partnerships and Family Life 165

Life Stages 188

When Life Gets Even Harder 204

Wrapping It Up 219

References 223

Index 225

Part 1

Autism,
Giftedness,
and Potential

Autistic and Gifted

I N THE 1990s, the term "2e," standing for "twice exceptional," was coined to describe individuals who were both intellectually or creatively gifted and had one or more dis/abilities. The term is a broad descriptor, as it covers any type of giftedness and every dis/ability. The terms "dual" or "multiple exceptionality" are sometimes used as well.

In this book, I have focused on a subset of the 2e population, those who are gifted and autistic. I want to write with respect to autistic culture and identity, and support that it is something you *are*, not something you *have*. I also wish to uphold the idea that humans have a spectrum of capacity, and I fully own our right to define ourselves. Any use of labels is done for ease of reading. It does not reflect my acceptance of the widespread use of labeling as an accurate way to identify and treat people.

Both to accommodate a need to use a defining term, and to honor the people I am describing, I will make up a term, "2eA," and use it in this book to represent gifted people who are also autistic. This is not meant to disrespect the identity of autistic people or to apply yet another label to a marginalized community; but 2e people who are also autistic are featured in this work, and using "2eA" increases readability. It is my hope that this term will carry an identifier, without the baggage of pathology or disrespect.

Characteristics of 2eA People

Many people with autism tend to underestimate their own gift-edness and may feel like imposters in the gifted world. Having an exceptional skill or ability that falls outside the typical definitions of giftedness can make it hard to recognize yourself as gifted. The world may only see gifted in academics or achievements; but there are many types of giftedness and various ways to express it. I hope the list below will help 2eA people to better recognize their gifts and abilities, whatever form they take.

As with any comprehensive list of characteristics, these char-acteristics are not shared by all 2eA people. It is difficult to place characteristics in "ability" and "dis/ability" or "strengths" and "weaknesses" categories, because oftentimes what could be con-sidered a weakness in one setting might be considered a strength in another. While it is difficult to codify individual characteristics, this list could be useful in providing a framework for identifying 2eA individuals.

Intellectual

- highly curious, divergent thinking
- intellectually advanced, good memory
- insatiable need for information
- learns "systems" to a high degree of competency
- detail-oriented
- can see obscure connections not easily seen by others
- advanced creativity and imagination
- strong metacognitive (thinking about their thinking) skills
- unique insight into complex issues

- have different, often surprising perspectives
- like to explore specific, often esoteric, subjects
- can rapidly accelerate learning to high levels of expertise
- extraordinary perceptions and/or abilities in one or more areas
- long attention span when working in areas of high interest
- may have difficulty with auditory instructions/learning
- very motivated to achieve mastery, may abandon subject due to perfectionism/unrealistic expectations
- persistent hyper-focus, often to the exclusion of all else
- asynchronous intellectual development
- are likely proud of intellect because it may be one of the few areas of success/recognition
- may also have learning dis/abilities.

Physical

- issues with food, multiple food aversions, need for eating rituals
- problems with digestion, gut health, food allergies
- sensory-processing issues
- can be hypersensitive to touch, often do not like to be touched; conversely, may be hyposensitive to touch, and seek rough physical interaction
- extremely sensitive to stimuli
- unusual sleep cycles, difficulty sleeping, less need for sleep

- trouble controlling body movements, movements may be awkward/clumsy
- trouble with modulating voice levels
- difficulty with personal hygiene and managing personal care
- may not be aware of physical sensations or needs (forget to eat, drink, sleep, go to bathroom)
- even if appearing chaotic or messy, need underlying system of order and routine
- may have weak muscle tone, poor gross motor skills, or asynchronous physical development.

Emotional

- empathetic
- deeply connect to those they love
- nonjudgmental, respectful of others
- intense feelings, may be confused by their emotions
- loyal and honest
- asynchronous emotional development
- overwhelmed by others' emotions and emotional intensity
- may have existential sorrow/depression
- perfectionist
- compulsive, obsessive
- impulsive
- have issues with anxiety, phobias
- unrealistic expectations of themselves

- low self-esteem, feel like an imposter
- emotional response out of sync with what is typical
- rigid about rules and fairness, struggle with gray areas, inflexibility
- may need time to prepare for changes to routine, surprises may be difficult for them to manage
- arrogant, or may appear arrogant
- may fall apart under pressure, hypervigilant
- trouble with understanding facial expressions and body language
- may struggle to communicate their feelings and understand the feelings of others.

Social

- often feel lonely, out of sync with others
- asynchronous social development
- concern for social justice
- may have a deep understanding of world problems and social injustice
- care deeply about the future of the world
- questioning of status quo, come up with creative alternatives
- may have trouble with authority; can be oppositional and argumentative
- adhere to rules and may be harsh on rule-breakers
- difficulty recognizing and responding to social rules

- may have high social anxiety, especially in unstructured activities
- blunt, literal, honest responses to queries, may assume others do not lie
- hate small talk and may have difficulty with rhetorical questions or polite responses
- comments and actions are out of sync with what others are doing
- may struggle to express themselves verbally
- gullible, socially awkward, often bullied and manipulated
- often misunderstood, ostracized
- confused by social protocol
- will be able to socialize more easily if they are in their safe and comfortable spaces.

Content Warning: This book describes situations and experiences that might be difficult to read, as it contains some descriptions of past institutional abuses and harming of marginalized people.

Labels Don't Define Me

———⬥———

IN MY LIFE and work as a neurodivergent woman, I have had to mask up to fit in many times. I've had to act less intelligent, tamp down my intensity, and hold back my empathy. I can't count the times I've stuffed myself into my normal suit, just to make others feel more comfortable. Yet, I also recognize my own privilege as an educated, white, middle-class, cisgendered woman. I have not experienced intersectional prejudice at the same level as many others in our neurodivergent community.

We've all heard that opposites attract; but at a deeper level, what we are searching for is someone who feels like home. We want to be able to be ourselves and find friends and lovers who accept us without reserve; but, for neurodivergent people, this can be challenging. Societies are built around upholding a particular community's established cultural norms. People who don't follow those norms are marginalized in many ways. They often experience bias across several aspects of who they are, a combined discrimination against race, intellect, gender, or sexuality. Those who hold power are likely to pathologize and label anyone whose lives and actions don't match their rules and values.

Rarely are marginalized people recognized as having an equally valid and empowered culture of their own. They are not valued unless they contribute to the power or wealth of those in control. In many societal bureaucracies, conformity and compliance are rewarded, individuality and nonconformity are not. Occasionally, creative, talented rule-breakers become powerful enough to have their differences tolerated; but, for the majority of marginalized people, life is not as accommodating. To blend in, they must mask their true identity and utilize compensatory strategies to fit in. Day in and day out, this gets to be exhausting and dehumanizing.

In nearly two decades of working among the "atypical," I have been deeply moved by the courage and tenacity of my community. We keep trying to bring our authentic selves forward, despite the many obstacles normalcy throws in our path. There is no well-marked life highway for neurodivergent travelers. Most of us careened off into the jungle when we were very young. We have spent our lives trying to hack out trails that will get us to our destinations, but the work is not easy. I have worked hard to be a trailblazer for my community, and even created some guidebooks along the way. My work has always been about gathering and sharing the wisdom of all those who have helped me explore this jungle.

When I first started doing research within the neurodivergent community, we were considered rare birds. There was not too much understanding of the population, and those who were doing research were not aware of, or connecting with, each other. We didn't have labels to fully describe our unique community, as the words "neurodivergence" or "twice exceptional" had not yet been coined or defined. We were sometimes described as "the gifted handicapped," then as "gifted with learning dis/abilities." The terms "Asperger's" and "autism spectrum" became more well known, but no descriptor completely encapsulated the community's experiences.

As researchers began to acknowledge that gifted intellect and dis/ability can manifest in many ways, the term "twice exceptional" (or "2e") began to circulate among academics. Eventually the definitions of twice exceptionality and neurodivergence began to disseminate into the public vocabulary and resonated with those who lived it. However, the medical and therapeutic communities did not (and still do not) utilize these terms diagnostically. Some clinicians who specialize in working with 2e and neurodivergent people will use them in their descriptions, but not in official diagnosis.

This can have an impact on many aspects of your life. If you don't have a diagnosis, you may not be able to access care or have your treatment covered by insurance. Your diagnosis might have labels that you don't feel apply to you or encapsulate your experience, but you have to accept them in order to qualify for help. Having an expert label you with something that doesn't feel authentic can be confusing, invalidating, and hurtful. It can also create a path of treatment protocols that don't actually help you and could even cause harm.

How others refer to you matters, as language is a powerful predictor of opportunity, treatment, and recognition. Mislabeling is a form of dismissal and control by those who hold power within the system. A great deal of work has been done by marginalized groups to define themselves and their experiences through language. They have regained power through reclaiming words and pushing back on how they are used. Controlling the narrative allows the story to be rewritten in a more neurodivergent-friendly way.

Professionals require a formal diagnosis before they label someone as autistic, but people have the right to label themselves too. Formal assessment is difficult for many people to schedule or afford. They could go years without diagnosis or may never get one. Yet, they have done extensive research on their own and know what feels true to them. Studying common traits and experiences can confirm what they have known about themselves from childhood. They may know long before formal diagnosis that they are 2eA.

However, I also want to recognize that, for many people, getting a diagnosis of autism and giftedness can be a relief. It can put a name to what they have been experiencing and give them a community and access to much needed information. Many people do not get diagnosed until they are well into adulthood. While this does not provide identification or accommodation soon enough to help in school or college, it can still be a support for adults, both on the job and in their personal life. There are common traits recognized and codified for diagnosis that can give you a starting point; but each person is a unique individual. Lists of traits may resonate, but not everything is reflected in a 2eA person's lived experience.

Diagnosis can give you language to inform neurotypical people about your profile and help them understand the autism/giftedness spectrum. It may even help them recognize that every 2eA individual will manifest their abilities and needs in their own unique way. For neurodivergent people, a diagnosis can validate their experiences and help them identify common challenges. It can also build understanding of how expectations or environments can hinder engagement and functionality. Diagnosis, and the accompanying labels and definitions, belong to the individual. Whether or not you choose to accept and disclose your label is a personal decision that should be respected by everyone.

It is also important for other people to use a person's chosen label, or to refrain from labeling if preferred, even if they don't have an official diagnosis. How we describe ourselves is an integral part of our identity formation. People have the right to describe and identify their experiences in ways that are true to themselves. For neurodivergent people, this is the essential foundation we build the rest of our lives on. We can begin to use inclusive language within our own community and model how to talk about ourselves to others. Some people want to be referred to using identity-first labels, such as *twice-exceptional people*, and others prefer person-first labeling, such as *a person with autism*. In this book I use both preferences, because honoring how people wish to be labeled is a crucial form of respect. Amy Sequenzia, an autistic author, discusses the impact of terminology in her work (Sequenzia, 2016). She notes that telling someone how they should define themselves is ableist; as it assumes a role of patronizing authority, particularly when it comes from outside the culture.

Non-autistic people have created many terms to define autistic and 2e people, and most of them do not reflect our cultural identity. For example, the term "high functioning" was used to describe autistic people who had above-average IQs. It is a label that has been rejected by the autistic community as inaccurate and insulting. Functionality is not correlated with IQ levels, as we don't live in an unchanging environment. Some people with autism may be *more functional* in some aspects of their lives than others, depending on the situation or environment. They may be *less functional* moment-to-moment depending on the demands and stressors placed on them. If we use "high functioning" as a label to describe IQ it becomes a hierarchical designation that insinuates a linear measurement, which is not a great way to describe a multi-dimensional mind.

Using IQ testing as a measurement of ability can be problematic as well, since dis/abilities or functionality issues can make it difficult to demonstrate actual intelligence levels on an assessment. For many 2e people, difficulties with working memory or processing speed may result in very low scores in those areas. That can impact the overall IQ score and inaccurately rate intelligence; but when an assessment report is written, it carries the professional weight of official descriptors. There is a bias toward professional outsider labels as being more correct, particularly if they come from scientific or academic research; but insider terms are likely to be more accurate to the experience of their community. For example, qualifying a person's expression of their own experiences as a *disorder* does not fairly or accurately represent their human qualities. As the neurodivergent community gains power, they can redefine their labels and determine how their experiences are identified and codified, both within and without their community.

Learning Firsthand

❖❖❖

A s a 2e person, I have been an ally of the autistic community for nearly 20 years. I have not achieved my career in a predictable way. It has been a long climb and I didn't really get a foothold until my late 40s. I began my career as a public-school teacher and suffered through a bureaucratic experience that dehumanized both me and my students. I reached a point where I could no longer follow a curriculum and educational model that I knew was harming many children.

I saw so many *atypical* children suffer harm within the traditional school model through gross ignorance about their needs, abilities, and sensitivities. When I just couldn't do it anymore, I resigned and began to work as an educational consultant specializing in supporting neurodiverse children and families. This role allowed me to advocate for their needs and help others to recognize their strengths. I attended many EHCP (Education, Health, and Care Plan) meetings, observed in multiple classrooms, and evaluated a number of programs and schools. I saw a great deal of trauma inflicted by professionals, both inadvertently and overtly. The 2e children carried these deep and pervasive wounds, and so did their parents through trying to protect and heal their children.

Working with these children and families was a daily reminder of my own hopes and plans. But years of trying to start a family had not been successful. As my 30s passed by, my husband and I decided to see an infertility specialist. After a few painful years of infertility and disappointment, I finally got pregnant. We were ecstatic to find out I was pregnant with twins; a lifetime dream was on its way to being realized! But things were not destined to go smoothly for me. I had to make some hard choices, and endure professional judgment early on, as I began to experience the role of parent-advocate firsthand. As a 41-year-old first-time mother (medically labeled as an *elderly* primigravida), I began to have complications. One of the babies was diagnosed with fetal growth restriction and my doctors advised me to allow a *selective reduction* (a procedure to abort the smaller fetus) to reduce the risk to myself and the other fetus. But I already felt fiercely protective of this smaller twin and, after weighing all of the risks, decided to keep both babies.

It was a difficult pregnancy, and the doctors' concerns were realized, as I spent nearly two months in the hospital struggling with an enlarged heart and fluid-filled lungs. My babies struggled too, the smaller twin did not grow adequately, and her placenta was failing. The larger baby had the cord wrapped around his neck several times and the doctors were concerned about oxygen deprivation. After I told one of the doctors that I had a gut feeling that both babies would be okay, he reiterated the gravity of the situation every time he made his weekly rounds. He seemed to think I was naïve and unable to accept reality. While he may have been trying to prepare me for the possibility of tragedy, I felt judged and shamed for not following his selective reduction advice.

The twins were born six weeks prematurely, and our parenting work began. We spent the first few weeks of their lives in a neonatal intensive care unit, not sure if they would both survive. I was determined to provide every possible opportunity I could give them, which became the hallmark of my parenting experience. When they were finally released from the hospital, we were placed in a program designed to follow premature babies' development and provide resources and support as needed. The clinic identified issues as they arose and offered assessments, diagnoses, and programs to help. As they grew, my son experienced significant speech and motor delays and my daughter had life-threatening health challenges.

I spent the first two years of their lives enveloped in fear—feeling vulnerable, and terrified of doing something wrong, I absorbed the information given to me by the professionals and tried my best to follow through with their recommendations. But as my twins reached preschool age, I began to question the experts. While I didn't doubt their original diagnoses of autism and developmental delays at that time, I didn't trust their approach to *treatment*. I felt the experts were not truly seeing my children. They checked boxes and formulated plans based on those clinical observations, but they missed so much.

We tried to point out that there were some remarkable things about our children. The professionals made notes when we told them our son, Dylan, was reading before age 2 and obsessively loved shapes and numbers. Or that our daughter, Morgan, was extremely empathetic, and a gifted storyteller who possessed a stunning vocabulary. But from their first year on, the professionals' focus was on the dis/abilities and providing early intervention to try to mitigate those *deficits*.

My husband and I decided to do the opposite and focus on their strengths. We didn't ignore that they struggled in some areas: Dylan has sensory-processing disorder (SPD), generalized anxiety disorder (GAD), social behavior and communication difficulties, auditory-processing problems, and working-memory issues. Morgan has dyslexia, dyscalculia, and GAD. They are also intellectually gifted and highly creative. From the beginning, our approach was to support without reservation and try to find ways to go around the dis/ability roadblocks. Rather than working on reforming behaviors to match the demands of a school program, we decided to try to find an environment that reduced stressors and increased opportunities to explore and learn.

In my previous work as a consultant, I had experienced

difficulty in finding schools that addressed the needs of neuro-diverse children, so I knew I would have the same challenge for my own children. We looked at multiple schools, always hoping that we might find a good fit. But, the closer we looked, the more we realized that most of the schools did not actually do what they advertised. We finally decided to just try out public school, but my children were bullied and began to have extreme anxiety about going to school. Ultimately, we decided to homeschool Morgan and Dylan, and that proved to be a healing experience for everyone. Our first years at home were filled with creativity, intense curiosity, playful exploration, and the sheer joy of pure learning.

I felt a great sense of freedom in knowing we didn't have to follow a standard curriculum or make them conform to behavioral expectations. If Dylan wanted to jump and flap his hands when he was excited by something, he wouldn't get in trouble for getting out of his seat. If Morgan wanted to tell a long and detailed story, she would not be restricted by the directions on the worksheet or be scolded for talking in class. Their schooling was not restricted by standards designed for a more typical student, and in many ways they thrived.

But as we began our third year of homeschooling, Morgan was longing for more interaction with other children. They had regular play dates, outings, and park days, but I realized she had a deep need for close friendships, which can be hard to sustain if you only see your friends once or twice a week. I knew I would have to create a way for her to have daily interaction with a group of friends. Even though I knew it would likely be futile, we looked again at a variety of schools, including Montessori, Waldorf, and gifted programs. Once again, we didn't find anything that seemed like it would work well for my children.

In desperation, I decided to try to design a school for kids like mine. Creating a school had never been something I considered doing, but necessity is the mother of invention! My goal was to form a community of true peers who shared common traits and gifts. I wanted the students to be mentored by compassionate adults who understood them holistically. It needed to be a place where 2e students could work to their strengths and satisfy their desire for deep exploration of chosen topics. I knew the school must allow students to fully be themselves and feel confident that they were safe, surrounded by adults who would help them when they were overwhelmed or anxious. Those adults would need to be specifically trained in dealing with fight-or-flight trauma response, recognizing compensatory coping behaviors, and providing stable, predictable, loving responses (Herman, 2015).

I drew on all of my past experience and combined it with the parental drive to protect my children. We started as a small "lab" school of ten children and met in my home. I wanted to try a practical application of my doctoral research about what 2e children needed at school. This resulted in the creation of "Big Minds," a school lovingly built for 2e children. This has allowed me to change the educational paradigm for our students. We have helped many 2e children over the years, focusing on their strengths and interests, while rejecting negative labels that may be based on previous behaviors or inaccurate diagnoses.

I often found the descriptive diagnoses and defined behaviors to be vastly inadequate and inaccurate in describing the actual child. We saw many individualized educational plans that carried judgmental labels like "emotionally disturbed" or "oppositional defiant disorder," when the actual issues were related to the child's sensitivities to their environment. When faced with documentation, and the requirement to understand behaviors, I always chose to base my beliefs about the child on what the child showed me directly. I found that neurodivergent children are often quite self-aware and intuitive.

In addition to giftedness, some of the most common diagnoses given to 2e children are autism, obsessive compulsive disorder (OCD)/GAD, attention deficit hyperactivity disorder (ADHD), SPD, nonverbal learning disorder (NLVD), social behavior and communication deficits, processing-speed difficulties, and executive-functioning issues. These cognitive and behavioral challenges are often combined with high empathy and sensitivity, as well as overexcitability[1] to stimulation. Sometimes, the diagnosis matches the person's experience; sometimes, it doesn't. Many 2e people choose to identify or label themselves with what feels most true to their experience.

When he was 17, my son was diagnosed as autistic in two of four defining categories; but identifies as 2e. He doesn't feel he experiences the world in an autistic way. Many 2e people with autism feel they belong to both the autistic and the 2e communities. Others may choose one identifier, or none at all. I respect my son's right to identify himself and align with whatever community resonates most with him. I am autism positive and 2e positive. I love my community and fully champion neurodivergent people.

My children are now adults and living their own private lives. I have their permission to talk about their childhood, but their stories are now theirs to tell. My story continues as I am expanding my work with my community. I am now completing hours to become a licensed therapist/counselor. My goal is to create further understanding and support for our neurodivergent community through a therapeutic lens. I continue my work as an advocate and educator because we still have a shortage of practitioners who understand the needs of neurodivergent people.

I find that so many fellow professionals are often too willing to find evidence of mental disorder in the normal lives and behaviors of neurodivergent people. They sometimes overlook the impact of living at the levels of creative, emotional, sensory, and intellectual intensity that most of us experience. Few practitioners receive training in identifying and supporting the complex needs of our community. Too often we are prescribed medications or therapies

---

1   From Dabrowski's Theory of Positive Disintegration, overexcitabilities are heightened sensitivities and responses to the environment (Dabrowski, 1964).

that take no account of our higher levels of awareness, sensitivity, and internal processes. We need to work with professionals who genuinely value our experiences and self-knowledge and strive to develop cultural competency for working with neurodivergent people.

For all the above listed reasons, I am not particularly comfortable with labeling people based on how they think and function, but humans have done so for centuries and it is encoded in our language. We often use pathologizing labels in efforts to categorize a problem and determine an approach to treatment. While that may be necessary in discussing a disease that requires a precise set of lifesaving protocols, it becomes much more problematic when we try to describe humans and all of their individualized behaviors. Using descriptors and language that comes from within the community is the first step toward honoring individuals and their reality. What you say matters.

Powerful Words

———◆◆◆———

Language structures our reality and impacts how we react to people and situations. For many people, diagnostic labels carry a negative connotation about their capacity and value. Historically, labels have often been used as justification for prejudice and abuse. In the mid-1800s, enslaved African Americans were diagnosed with *drapetomania*, a "mental illness" that caused enslaved people to want to escape from captivity. Or more recently, *excited delirium* has been used to describe a "mental condition" that causes people to fight physical restraint by police officers, even if that restraint is causing harm. Using the term "excited delirium" to rationalize restraint, and subsequent forced sedation, is disproportionately used against African Americans (one of the many injustices currently being protested by groups like Black Lives Matter in the U.S.).

Women's behaviors throughout history have also been pathologized and dismissed as *hysteria*, without consideration for their personal experiences. Hysteria was used diagnostically until the 1950s when the American Psychiatric Association finally dropped the term from the *Diagnostic and Statistical Manual of Mental Disorders* (DSM: APA, 2013).[1] However, the prejudice related to women's

---

1   A manual used by all mental health professionals in the United States to diagnose mental illness.

mental health appears to have resurfaced under the term "Border-line Personality Disorder." This disorder is diagnosed 75 percent more often among women than men and has echoes of hysteria in its definition.

Autistic people have also experienced intolerance and denigration within the medical/therapeutic community. In the 1940s psychiatrists began to use psychological instruments to assess mental and emotional capacity, a process that is highly subjective and susceptible to cultural norms. Psychiatrists wanted to increase their ability to categorize people with pathological identifiers, so began to utilize medical examinations to measure physical aspects of development and identify pervasive behaviors that might be considered markers for autism. They noted that there were differences in how autistic people interacted with their environment and related to others, and these differences were pathologized as deficits.

For example, they began to define speech patterns as *echolalia*, interactions with others as *extreme autistic aloneness*, and behaviors as *obsessive repetitiousness to complex, nonsense patterns* (Kanner, 1943). Diagnostic criteria were needed to enact laws that would allow bureaucracies the legal and financial backing to design education and treatment protocols. However, these protocols further codified people with autism as deficient.

In many cultures around the world, such people were labeled as *psychotic, unmanageable, ineducable, feeble-minded, possessed*, and *morally defective*. Autistics were experimented on and treated without respect to their rights, safety, or humanity. In a U.K. parliamentary hearing in 1960, the children in these experimental treatments were unashamedly defined as follows:

> These children are apparently schizoids who live in a dream world. They seem intelligent, but it is impossible to touch them even with treatment that is nowadays giving success in 75 percent of normal adult schizoids. (Carr, 1960, col. 1443)

Many so-called "treatments" have been used to alter or control "autistic" behaviors. Autistic people have been experimented on and have suffered through the following "therapies": insulin shock therapy (injecting insulin, which can cause subarachnoid hemorrhage and death), electroconvulsive therapy (an electric pulse is sent through the brain and can cause loss of brain function, memory, and identity), aversive punishment therapy (administering electric shocks when the child does not adhere to behavioral standards), applied behavior analysis (ABA) therapy (a method of behavioral training using rewards for compliance and punishments for noncompliance), parentectomy (removing the child from their parents for extended periods of time because they believed that autism was caused by cold, unresponsive mothers), holding therapy (physical restraint and forced eye contact, which can be physically and emotionally traumatic), drugs such as LSD and Lupron (administered without consideration for long-term side-effects), and parent-administered treatments such as Miracle Mineral Solution (a solution of the disinfectant sodium chlorite, in distilled water, which is administered orally or via an enema). Most of these "treatments" were undertaken without consent, as children and those considered mentally incapable are not given a choice.

While most of these "therapies" have been discontinued, some are still in practice, such as electroconvulsive therapy, which has limited use, and ABA therapy, which is considered standard care and used extensively. It is not my intention to demonize past researchers and practitioners, as I do not know their motivations for their work; but I do condemn continuing to disregard the experiences and protests of people on the autism spectrum who have decried these treatments as damaging. We often look at the work of historical practitioners as barbaric, and I fear that, decades forward, our current therapeutic, social, and behavioral approaches to 2eA people will also seem destructive and dehumanizing.

Much more detailed descriptions of the perceived causes and recommended treatments of autism used since the 1930s can be found in books such as Adam Feinstein's *A History of Autism:*

Conversations with the Pioneers, or in Chloe Silverman's *Understanding Autism*; but many feel books like these do not adequately reflect the voices of autistic people themselves. As a unique culture within many other cultures, people with autism are impacted by the larger societal norms and customs. Worldwide, there is no universal description, diagnosis, or treatment protocol that is utilized. In one society, autism might be seen as a developmental disorder, in another a mental illness, some regard it as a spiritual possession, and others may see it as a punishment from God.

There are a few cultures, such as the Navajo/Dine'é nation (Kapp, 2011), who typically embrace autism as a state of being, a distinct expression of individuality and personhood. When groups of people don't pathologize autism, people with autistic differences are simply embraced as a legitimate part of the larger culture. Unfortunately, in most cultures, autistic people are a marginalized group, and have been historically silenced by the institutionalized approach to identification and treatment. If we continue to look at autism through the pathological lens of dis/ability, we are missing the true picture. It is imperative that we listen to the experiences and concerns of people on the spectrum, as their firsthand wisdom will be key to developing a deep understanding of their strengths and challenges. Only then will we be able to design programs, spaces, and approaches that allow autistic people to bring their authentic selves forward without reserve or restriction.

Like the autistic community, twice exceptional people have long been misunderstood and their needs overlooked. It was not until 1972 that the U.S. Congress first had discussions on educating children who were gifted and had learning dis/abilities. While a report warned that "gifted and talented children are, in fact, deprived and can suffer psychological damage and permanent impairment of their abilities to function well" if not given appropriate accommodations, there was still a reluctance to see them as a special-needs population (Marland, 1972).

It was not until the 1980s that the conversation began to include the idea that a person could be both gifted and have learning dis/abilities. For the next two decades, the recognition of 2e students and discussion of their needs resurfaced quite regularly, but nothing was actually done to meet them. Finally, in 2005, the IDEA (Individuals with Disabilities Education Act) in the U.S. officially acknowledged that 2e students exist. In fact, they estimated that between 6 and 8 percent of disabled students in the public school system are also gifted, yet the IDEA did not go so far as to require identification or accommodation of their needs.

Twice exceptional students cannot be appropriately educated if they are placed in special education to accommodate their dis/ability, nor will their dis/abilities be adequately supported if they are placed in a gifted program alone. They may use their high intellect to develop compensatory strategies that allow them to function as an average student in a regular classroom, but those achievement levels will not accurately reflect their abilities. Many teachers and administrators have little understanding of the emotional, physical, and mental toll these compensatory efforts take on a child who is 2e. They are often seen as lazy, defiant, and disruptive, while there is no awareness that they are suffering. School can be a very traumatic place for 2e students, and many spend their entire day in a constant state of fight or flight.

The majority of 2e students struggle for years in the classroom without recognition or support. All too often, their needs are only addressed when they begin to have severe behavioral problems or start to fall significantly behind academically. Sadly, parents often lack information about twice exceptionality as well, so may turn to teachers and other professionals for help. If those professionals don't understand what it means to be 2e, or how to appropriately support these children, they can increase the suffering through misplaced efforts and inaccurate labels. I have seen many 2e children who are experiencing daily trauma (and reacting to that trauma the only way they know how), only to be punished for their behaviors.

Many of them are given terrible labels such as "emotionally disturbed," "oppositional defiant disorder," or "pathological demand avoidance." I have had many conversations with parents who see their child come home hurt and discouraged from school each day. When they turn to professionals for help, they are told that the child, or the way they parent their child, is the problem. Imagine watching your child become so chronically stressed that they can only relate to the world through aggression or withdrawal; and then be told by those in charge that your child is emotionally disturbed. So many parents of 2e children are also traumatized by the hardship of trying to advocate for their children, helping them regulate their behavior, and then dealing with the fallout.

In my work with 2e children at school, I have seen children crawl into lockers, hide under desks, or burrow behind furniture in an effort to find a space where they felt safe. They also become selectively mute, dissociate, pass out, or run away. Those behaviors happen with children whose nervous systems are in a *freeze* or *flight* state. When they are in *fight* mode they scream, swear, bite, hit, and kick. They will often weaponize anything within reach as they try to equalize power. I've heard children threaten to harm or kill themselves and others, often in graphic and creative ways. All this comes from enduring chronic stress and trauma in a school setting.

Yet, teachers and parents alike are often only focused on how these behaviors prevent their child (and others) from learning. They work to figure out how to get the child back on track academically but overlook or underestimate the emotional damage. When these children stray too far beyond acceptable behavior, they are often punished, shamed, isolated, and medicated. Dr. Ross Greene, a well-known advocate for behaviorally struggling/challenged children, wants people to understand that *all* behavior is a form of communication. It is the job of the adults in the room to find out why the behavior is happening and help the child to get their needs met in a more appropriate way.

If we used this approach with children from the beginning,

particularly those who are labeled *atypical*, we would not have so many neurodivergent adults working to reverse the damage done to them in childhood. I am staggered by the pain and loss of potential that is part of life for so many 2eA people. Because humans tend to hold on to what has always been done, 2eA people have to work much harder to achieve their personal goals. There is often a significant disparity between the 2eA person's desires, and what the world is willing to accommodate. Work, relationships, householding, and recreation can be painfully difficult, particularly because most 2eA people's talents and capacities are not valued or are masked by dis/abilities.

Being an Advocate

I F YOU WERE LABELED as having a deficit when you were a child, and had a significant focus placed on therapies to fix you, it is likely that you didn't feel very competent or confident. If those in charge of your growing experiences did not validate you, it is difficult to feel a high degree of self-worth. When parents, teachers, doctors, and therapists tell you that your behaviors and life view are not acceptable, you end up feeling alienated.

I have provided support to many 2eA people who are disheartened and disillusioned by the system they are forced to embrace. They expend an incredible amount of energy trying to do what is "right" with their partners, children, friends, and bosses. There is an expectation that they will be able to assimilate into the mainstream culture of a neurotypical world. The responsibility is on them to figure out how to make it all work, without expecting others to accommodate their needs or eccentricities. Many feel like they are imposters in their own lives, particularly if they need to mask their differences on a daily basis. To complicate matters, there is not nearly enough expert support from medical, therapeutic, academic, and business/corporate professionals who truly understand.

I can appreciate that many professionals are trying to find ways to improve outcomes for 2eA people, particularly children; and I know there are those who have devoted their lives to research and activism. However, most researchers and practitioners are not part of the neurodivergent culture and have not lived the experience of those who are 2e/autistic. I believe that the most impactful movement toward change comes from within the 2eA community. For example, the only reason that autism is no longer officially classified as a form of schizophrenia in the DSM is due to autistic person/parent activism and a few open-minded professionals.

Many enlightened mental health practitioners consider the DSM to be a blunt instrument at best, and they believe it should be used with caution. Rather than pathologizing classes of behaviors, we should enquire how people interact with their environments and find the root cause of any distress. Treatment then becomes more about finding ways for the environment to work for the person, and less about making the person change to meet the requirements of the environment.

Grassroots organizations, such as the Autistic Self Advocacy Network[1] (whose tagline is "Nothing About Us Without Us") and Mad in America (see identity article by Dana Holmes, a 2eA person: Holmes, 2020), or educational platforms such as Yo Samdy Sam, The Aspie World, Purple Ella, and Autistic Tyla on YouTube, are critical to building understanding and compassion for the very real differences that, when overlooked or misunderstood, can create problems and impede functioning.

Most of the difficulties faced by 2eA people lie with how their societies view them. They are wounded by cultural limitations and expectations. Industrialized Western nations have attempted to assimilate marginalized cultures through ethnocide and colonialism for centuries. In the case of autistic culture, the value of the cultural identity has been overshadowed by the desire to *cure* the *disease*. Rather than focusing on improving the quality of life for disenfranchised communities, those in power continually seek to subjugate, exploit, or eradicate noncompliant or undervalued groups of people. To fully recognize the potential of all people, we

---

1   https://autisticadvocacy.org

need to build a society that recognizes the value of *all* people; one that is willing to embrace and accommodate a broader spectrum of human experience and expression.

While I can appreciate the growing number of autism-friendly workplace or school-based programs, they are often still focused on how the 2eA person can provide benefit to the company or school, rather than how to give each individual adequate and appropriate support. Expecting that all autistic job applicants are great with coding or detail-oriented work, and then placing value on the person through that lens, is biased. It ignores the fact that 2eA people have multiple abilities, needs, and interests. A truly inclusive environment would find out what each individual needs, rather than ticking the boxes on a blanket checklist of possible accommodations. I am working toward the day when 2eA people can bring their authentic selves into an environment, and find a community that understands and embraces them wholeheartedly.

This book is a form of activism, a small contribution toward building a more egalitarian life. It is designed both to celebrate the talents, humor, creativity, and intellect of 2eA people, and to help those outside the community better understand the realities of life as a 2eA person. The experiences of 2eA people are equally valid and should be universally honored. We should feel pride in our neurodiversity, and advocate for others to do the same. 2eA voices should be the ones most prominently heard when we are deciding what it means to be a 2eA person. It takes a great deal of tenacity to keep trying to make others see your value, while still remaining true to yourself. This book tells insider 2eA stories that celebrate success and share compassionate coping strategies for overcoming and rethinking the tough parts.

Part 2

Stories

THE FOLLOWING STORIES are a fictional compilation of the lives and experiences of 2eA people I have known over the last two decades. I have attempted to create believable stories that will protect the real people's privacy, but also accurately reflect their characters, situations, behaviors, thoughts, and conversations. I have tried to create fictional representations that inform, but also honor and respect 2eA people's experiences overall.

2eA Grows Up

WHAT IS IT LIKE to be a 2eA in a neurotypical world? There are many common experiences in the lives of 2eA people, related to their overlapping giftedness and dis/abilities. Their gifts can mask dis/abilities, and the reverse is also true. Many 2eA people have never felt they can fit in or successfully navigate *normal* life. This can start when they are very young through early intervention therapies such as pragmatic speech (Parsons et al., 2017) or ABA, two common approaches that are designed to improve a 2eA child's communication and behavior. The problem with this approach is that it often does not honor the child's own attempts to communicate or make an effort to understand their actions. Some practitioners are very formulaic, and many 2eA people report that their experiences were often unhelpful, and, at worst, traumatic.

BeBe

This is the case for BeBe, a profoundly gifted, wickedly funny 2eA person. She has a round, jovial face with mischievous dark eyes and a ready smile, but she didn't feel happy very often growing up. BeBe's childhood experiences were an exercise in frustration and bewilderment. After an early diagnosis, her parents tried to be proactive and follow the recommended professional guidelines for speech therapy, social group work, ABA therapy, occupational therapy, mental health support, medication, and special education placement. BeBe spent all of her school days bored to distraction, unable to demonstrate her keen intellect. She was also confused by social norms, but had difficulty describing her reality. Teachers rarely accommodated her in ways that allowed her to utilize her gifts and appropriately meet her needs.

She often had similar experiences with medical and therapeutic professionals, even those who were trained in working with autistic children. For example, BeBe worked with a speech therapist who was teaching her about expressing emotions. The therapist showed BeBe cards illustrating various facial expressions one would make when experiencing a particular emotion. BeBe duly noted and memorized the crying face that indicated being sad, the smiling face for excitement, the glaring face for anger, and so on. She was told that when something happens to make you hurt or sad, like losing your favorite toy or falling and scraping your knee, you would cry. For BeBe this was a prescription for behavior, as she was desperately trying to interpret how neurotypical people experienced the world. "I remember thinking I was being given instructions. Okay, got it. If you're sad or hurt, you cry."

A few months later, five-year-old BeBe was at the pool for her swimming lesson. She jumped into the shallow end and felt a sharp sting on her heel. She looked down and was fascinated to see blood pumping out of her foot. She was so interested in what was happening that she didn't feel much pain. BeBe watched intently as the blood swirled and dissipated into the water like squid ink.

She leaned forward to get a better look and then realized the children around her were screaming. Her Dad yanked her out of the pool and ran to a nearby chair. After looking at the wound, he told her to hold very still, and then pulled out a large shard of glass. When he did, the blood began to flow more quickly. Her Dad shouted for someone to bring something to stop the bleeding. BeBe could see her Dad was upset, but she didn't feel upset. She was interested in what was happening. She began to investigate her cut in a scientific way, but then someone handed her Dad a towel and he wrapped her foot up tightly. When she saw the look of concern on her Dad's face, she remembered that when you are hurt, you cry. So BeBe began to cry. She cried loudly all the way to the hospital. She knew her Dad was concerned, and she wanted to make sure she did "sad" correctly. Nothing her Dad did consoled BeBe.

When they got to the emergency room, a nurse hurried BeBe and her Dad into an examination room. As the doctor began to look at her wound, her Dad turned her face the other way. BeBe began to cry louder and struggled to get out of his grasp. The nurse said she would have to hold BeBe so the doctor could administer anesthetic and stitch up her wound. The more they restrained her, the more BeBe fought and cried. They didn't know that she was struggling because she wanted to see what they were doing, not because she was hurt or afraid.

Finally, in desperation, her Dad told BeBe she had to stop fighting and crying. BeBe stopped immediately and then began to ask the doctor questions. "Why is blood red? Where did it come from? Why were they sewing the wound shut?" BeBe laughingly said, "I am sure they were shocked by the instant change in behavior, but it was probably just chalked up to autism weirdness." BeBe can laugh about it now, but she was often bewildered by others' actions, and hurt by their lack of understanding of her own.

BeBe said she wished that all the early efforts to teach her about emotions had not been so focused on causes and predicted behaviors, but had been more about what being sad or happy feels like inside. She recognizes that it can be difficult to describe what emotions feel like but believes you can describe the physical sensations and manifestations of differing emotional states. BeBe thinks that would have been much more useful.

She has been accused of not being empathetic to others' emotions because she doesn't respond to them in a neurotypical way. For example, when a classmate began to cry as she told the class her dog had died, BeBe felt a rush of intense emotion that was difficult to tolerate, so she began to laugh uncontrollably. Her teacher scolded her for being unkind and made her apologize to the other student. The teacher's assumption that BeBe is not empathetic was wrong. BeBe often feels too much and is overwhelmed by the experience. Trying to explain this in a way that resonates with neurotypical people can be very frustrating for BeBe and often makes her feel misjudged and excluded. "The sad truth is that I still have to explain my feelings and actions. I have been fighting this battle my whole life and it is depressing how little has changed."

BeBe's childhood was defined by her relentless efforts to be accepted, yet she was systematically rejected. She was bullied by both children and adults, ridiculed and excluded with horrifying regularity. BeBe remembers her feelings of bewilderment when she was publicly shamed by the teacher for talking with her first-grade classmates about how animals mate. The teacher told her they were not allowed to talk about "inappropriate" things at school. BeBe, who has always been a scientist at heart, could not comprehend what could possibly be inappropriate about the reproductive cycle. When her parents tried to explain why certain topics were off-limits at school, BeBe felt embarrassed that she didn't know this. It was just one more indicator that there must be something inherently wrong with her.

BeBe tried to emulate other children. She watched what they did and how they talked, trying to find a way to fit in. But she also recalls feeling really sad that she was expected to fit in with people who could be so unkind. BeBe witnessed many cruel interactions that went unnoticed by others. She was surprised to see which children were popular or who got rewards from the teachers. The most thoughtful children, or those who were consistently kind, were not always the ones rewarded. The social hierarchies and exclusions were confusing to her. BeBe knows that some social nuances have always been harder for her to see and interpret; but she also knows she has a strong sense of empathy and could always feel when someone did something hurtful.

She was frequently confused about why some children were seen as funny or clever, while others were rejected and ridiculed. BeBe said she has a clear memory of sitting at a lunch table and watching a group of boys laugh at each other as they made quiet fart noises when the lunch monitor moved to the other end of the lunchroom. BeBe wanted to join them, she thought she could be funny too. She tried to make the sounds with her hands as she saw the boys do but couldn't make it work. BeBe knew she could actually fart loudly, so she slid along the bench and forcibly farted. After a moment of shocked silence, the boys burst into peals of laughter. As the smell began to waft up, which coincided with the lunch monitor's arrival, the boys held their noses and called her "gross" and "disgusting."

The lunch monitor scolded BeBe and escorted her out of the lunchroom into the principal's office. BeBe had to eat lunch in his office for the rest of the week. She felt unfairly called out, isolated, and punished. She could not defend her actions because she couldn't find the words to tell the whole story. BeBe despaired that even if she could get the adults to listen, they still might not understand. She saw firsthand that adults are more prone to support the children whose personalities and behaviors aligned with their own.

Throughout her childhood, BeBe never felt that she was accepted. She experienced persistent rejection, being told that her way of being was not appropriate. BeBe said she felt gaslighted and disparaged for being her authentic self. "Going to school was awful. Being regularly pressured to conform, ridiculed, bullied, and rejected is traumatic." She knows she experiences many things differently than neurotypical people in a myriad of ways; but she doesn't think that gives them an excuse for ignorance and biased behavior. BeBe believes the world needs 2eA people to bring their own brand of normal to society and create a space where their experiences are respected. Those outside the 2eA community could also learn and grow from shifting their perspective.

BeBe remembers being shocked the first time a high school teacher recognized her talent and commended her on a self-directed project. BeBe's academic experience throughout childhood was mostly focused on learning to comply and submit to those in control. She found it hard to be intellectually gifted, but unable to show her abilities due to rigid curricula and ignorant teachers. BeBe was able to do well enough in school to progress through her grades and graduate, but it took substantial intervention from her parents to make it happen.

BeBe feels her parents made some mistakes, such as following strict ABA protocols and keeping her in special education throughout elementary school; but they also did many things right. When BeBe told her parents that she wanted to try homeschooling instead of going to middle school, they supported that decision. They recognized BeBe was not receiving appropriate intellectual stimulation at school and were willing to help her pursue her passions at home. They put their energies into finding resources and experiences for each of BeBe's areas of interest.

Her parents diligently searched to find professionals who had experience with 2eA children. If they couldn't find informed professional help, they educated themselves and tried to pass that knowledge along. Through efforts to support their daughter, they became informed advocates. This helped BeBe to feel less alone in the world. Even though they often struggled to figure out how best to support her, BeBe knew they were her staunch allies whom she could count on.

When BeBe was 15, she asked to enroll at a local high school. Her parents supported her there too. They advocated for appropriate accommodations, knowing that BeBe would need that to succeed. She did succeed, partly due to those accommodations, and partly to her intrinsic desire to reach her long-term goals. Perhaps the most important gift BeBe's parents gave her was their belief in her ability to figure out what she wanted to do. They struggled at many points in her life, but they followed her lead and focused on her strengths, which gave BeBe a safe place in the world. They also tried to stay open and curious about BeBe's journey and adopt or reject guidelines depending on what they could see was working for her. It was a learning process for BeBe's parents, but they didn't give up. She credits their tenacity and resilience for her current sense of mental well-being and functionality in the world.

As an adult, BeBe has more control over her life. She has gained the capacity to align her choices with what she values. She now has more freedom to find companions and activities that better suit her worldview. BeBe still has days where she struggles to make herself understood, and to accurately interpret her interactions with others; but, overall, she acknowledges that life is better as an adult.

BeBe has been able to find places where her strengths are an asset. Her intellect, love for science, and raw talent helped her shine academically and complete an advanced degree in biochemistry. She was able to develop a level of expertise that led to a satisfying career. BeBe is happily contributing her skills at a research firm and earning a good living. The firm has a reputation for creating an autism-friendly work environment, which includes reduced sensory stimuli, support around organizational functioning, and accommodation for social and communication demands. Most importantly, they asked BeBe what she needed to be comfortable and productive.

BeBe was delighted to find that there were other 2eA people at her firm and enjoyed being with co-workers who shared some of her interests and understood her innate worldview. Combined with supportive supervisors and company-wide sensitivity training, BeBe's career has formed the foundation for building a fulfilling life.

BeBe knows that such a strong foundation is not possible for a significant number of 2eA people, usually due to factors beyond their control. She has opportunities that many of her peers do not, and that is distressing to her. BeBe feels every 2eA person should have the chance to develop their strengths and passions from a young age. She strongly believes that there should be less focus on early intervention to train 2eA children out of their natural behaviors.

BeBe is adamant that children should be allowed to be themselves. "How can you develop your talents and abilities when all the adults around you are telling you that you are broken? I am amazed at how carelessly teachers and therapists dismissed my authenticity. No one asked me how I wanted to communicate, or what skills I wanted to develop. No one seemed curious to find out what I was good at or what makes me tick. It's just a wrong way to go about providing support."

Julian

Having the support of a caring adult, particularly as an advocate to help in stressful situations, can be a highly protective factor. Most trauma is experienced when one feels helpless and unable to protect oneself in any given situation. Many children with dis/abilities face daily trauma and are not able to articulate what is happening to them.

This was the case for Julian, a 2eA person whose childhood was traumatic. As a baby, he was very reactive to sounds and to being touched. His parents had difficulty soothing him and he didn't sleep well at night. He was a colicky baby and his pediatrician had concerns about his lack of adequate growth. Julian's parents had two older children, so felt they were experienced at child rearing, but most of their tried-and-true methods did not work for Julian.

As he grew, Julian began to have tantrums, sometimes several in a day. His father joked that he was stuck in the "terrible twos," but the length and extent of the tantrums were no laughing matter. Julian's cherubic face and blond curls gave no warning of his explosive temper. He could quickly become physically aggressive, hitting, kicking, biting, and throwing objects at anyone within range. His parents responded to the aggression by locking him in his bedroom for a "time out." By the time he was 5, Julian had damaged or destroyed most of the objects and furnishings in his bedroom.

When he started school, the aggression increased. Within the first month, Julian was sent home several times for hitting and kicking his classmates and the teacher. At the end of the first semester, his teacher referred him to the school psychologist for evaluation. The psychologist diagnosed him with autism and nonverbal learning disorder, but also noted that he scored in the gifted range in some areas of the assessment, namely his decoding proficiency, exceptional vocabulary, and strong rote memory skills. This diagnosis of his deficits synced with Julian's behaviors, now listed as *psychosocial difficulties* (emotional dysregulation, inability to interact with others appropriately, defiance and opposition). According to the school's established protocols, Julian's behaviors and challenges outweighed his areas of giftedness. The psychologist recommended he be moved to a special ed class for moderately disabled students.

Julian's parents agreed because they didn't know what else to do with him. They respected the professional expertise of the school staff and knew that Julian would not be able to stay in a regular classroom. His new class consisted of seven other children whose behaviors had disqualified them from inclusion in a general educational setting. His new teacher was supported by two aides who were trained in working with behaviorally challenged students, including methods of restraint and seclusion.

Julian's world at school became a living nightmare. The classroom was always noisy and there were daily physical altercations, as the aides often used restraint to ensure compliance with rules and stop fights. Julian became a regular target for discipline, often held in a seated or prone position by both aides. If he didn't settle down after restraint, he was locked in the "safe room" until he could calm down. The safe room was not safe for Julian. It was a small, dim, isolated space without furnishings, the school equivalent of a solitary confinement prison cell. Julian often spent hours of each day in isolation, alternating between screaming and fighting to be let out, and curled into a fetal position on the floor.

Julian's parents were not aware of the extent of the restraint and isolation, as his teacher did not report what was happening each day, and Julian could not adequately verbalize his levels of distress. He began to regularly hurt himself, biting his arms and legs, punching himself in the face, and pounding his head against the wall. In desperation, his parents took him to a psychiatrist for an evaluation. The doctor prescribed medication to reduce aggressive behaviors and help Julian be more emotionally regulated.

His aggressive behaviors at school improved, as the medication calmed him down and slowed his reactions and responses. Things were better for his parents at home too. Julian now fell asleep shortly after dinner and slept through the night. He was no longer argumentative or combative, and spent a great deal of his waking hours at home dozing or watching TV.

His mother expressed concerns to the psychiatrist, but reducing his medication caused his behavioral issues to return. His parents were worried about his lethargy, but also somewhat relieved to have a break from his aggression. His psychiatrist recommended working with a skilled behavioral therapist to help Julian learn better coping skills and his parents learn better parenting skills. They had a mutual goal to reduce his medication as he learned how to behave.

As Julian progressed through second grade, the work with the therapist helped improve his behavior. His therapist, Jess, had experience with neurodivergent children and was a compassionate well-informed practitioner. Most importantly, she had observed the classroom environment and could see that it was contributing to Julian's maladaptive behavior. Jess was able to get the school to provide a home-health option for six months, which allowed Julian to remain at home during the school day. Jess came to see him twice a week, and the school sent a teacher once a week to work with him at home. The teacher took time to get to know Julian and tried to bring work she thought he would be interested in doing. This one-on-one home support allowed him to begin to recover from the trauma of his previous classroom. Julian found comfort in the routine of working with his teacher and Jess at home, and his ability to express himself verbally also began to improve.

His parents learned how to recognize when he was becoming emotionally dysregulated and adopted strategies to calm Julian and help him feel safe. Eventually he became less reactive and more compliant. Over time, their mutual work allowed the psychiatrist to successfully reduce Julian's medication dosage. His aggression did not return; and because his behaviors had significantly improved, Jess thought he might be eligible to go back to a regular classroom.

At the beginning of third grade, Julian's parents lobbied to have him moved into a regular education classroom. Due to a policy of providing the least restrictive educational environment, Julian qualified to have his behavior re-evaluated. The school psychologist and behavioral specialist agreed that he should be moved out of his previous special education setting.

But school was still a daily chronic stressor for Julian, and he did not feel comfortable in the general education classroom. The larger classroom's noise and activity levels were nearly as overwhelming as his previous special ed classroom had been. Initially, Julian tried to leave the classroom, but when he was unable to physically escape, he found other ways to leave. He began to dissociate[1] and developed selective mutism. Julian often seemed to be lost in daydreaming and rarely spoke throughout the day. Rather than going into fight-or-flight defense, Julian was now quiet and cooperative,

---

1   Dissociation can include: amnesia; feeling disconnected from your body; feeling disconnected from the world; losing a sense of who you are; loss of feelings/emotions; or even losing control of your body.

but withdrawn and disengaged. It seemed that the only real benefit the regular classroom provided was not having to suffer from the restraint and isolation of previous years.

Julian's parents again met with the administrators to advocate for appropriate accommodations. They wanted to make sure he could reach his full potential at school, and felt he needed greater support. In a regular educational classroom, Julian's autism diagnosis and lack of academic progress qualified him for support from a one-to-one aide. The administration reluctantly agreed and new Education, Health, and Care Plan goals were written to address his needs.

His new aide, Rasha, was a calm and gentle person who was extraordinarily kind to Julian. She felt a compassionate connection to him, as her own son had been a disabled person. She had escaped with her son from a war in her homeland, but he had not survived the journey to the refugee camp. Rasha recognized a terrified child when she saw one. She worked hard to build Julian's trust and give him a sense of security. Rasha understood that people cannot learn when they are anxious and stressed; and she knew the physical signs of a person in fight-or-flight response. If Julian began to show signs of distress, they left the classroom and walked through the woodland park next to the school playground.

She knew that Julian was not a typical learner, so as they walked, she talked about the science of the woodlands or the beauty of mathematics in nature. While school personnel knew of his assessment scores, Rasha was the first to really recognize Julian's high intelligence. She began to work with him on his reading and found that he progressed very quickly. As his reading capacity grew, he spent a good part of his day reading books that were well above grade level. Rasha also found that Julian could focus on science experiments and science-related videos for long periods of time without assistance.

Julian was still easily startled and could quickly become upset when bothered by other students or when he was frustrated with his work. But Rasha's gentle and loving presence helped Julian feel safer and more relaxed. She stayed with Julian year-to-year as he moved through his elementary grades. By the time he was ready to begin middle school, Rasha had been able to validate Julian's giftedness, even though he still struggled to produce written work and keep up with homework. Over his elementary years, Rasha developed a relationship with Julian and his parents, and was an integral part of Julian's success.

When Julian began middle school, Rasha helped his parents to secure placement at a STEM-focused[2] public charter school. His new school was project-based and very hands-on, both areas of strength for Julian. He would also have daily support from a resource specialist, to help him complete assignments and build academic skills. Julian's parents also hired Rasha to work with him twice a week at home, to maintain consistency and stability.

Julian began to catch up academically, often impressing his teachers with his depth of knowledge on subjects of interest. While homework was still a struggle, Julian was able to finish his class assignments and score well on tests. When given a hands-on project, such as creating a science experiment or building a working model, Julian excelled. As his success grew, so did his confidence. Rasha's early recognition and understanding of his trauma gave her insight on how to help him cope with school-related stress. Her ongoing support enabled Julian to feel more capable of managing emotional and academic demands. Having a person who unconditionally accepted him, and recognized his unique way of being, was a key factor in his success.

Rasha helped Julian have confidence and develop a sense of self-worth. Julian felt that his parents loved him and knew they had worked hard to advocate for him in their own way. However, he also felt they had never truly understood the depth of what he was experiencing. He was grateful they had recognized how

2 Science, technology, engineering, mathematics (STEM).

much Rasha was able to help him and appreciated their efforts to maintain his connection with her over the years.

As Julian moved through his high-school years he developed the confidence to self-advocate. He could explain to teachers and fellow students that certain environmental experiences were stressful and reduced his ability to function. He was able to request accommodations that enabled him to accurately demonstrate his level of understanding. Julian became proficient at using technology to mitigate his weaknesses, such as speech-to-text for written assignments, and an organization app to help him with time management.

Julian was also creative in figuring out ways to manage his workload. He often listened to reading assignments at double speed and developed his own style of mind-mapping for taking notes. He realized that he was able to remember details and understand connections in ways that many did not. For the first time in his life, Julian felt he was intellectually gifted, and that his intellect could help overcome his deficits.

As he matured, Julian began to feel a desire to connect to his peers in ways he hadn't felt before. Rasha had been his primary friend throughout his elementary and middle-school years, and that had been enough at the time. But now that he was less overwhelmed by school, he felt he had the energy to try to make friends. While he found many of the social norms bewildering, he also discovered patterns of behavior that allowed him to predict possible outcomes and develop scripts. He learned to socialize in ways and places that were not overwhelming. By the time he graduated high school, Julian had a small circle of friends who shared his interests and accepted his differences.

Julian's personal growth and development, in both academic and social areas, was possible because his trauma was recognized and addressed effectively. While his parents and teachers had followed accepted treatment protocols, what helped Julian most was Rasha's recognition of his trauma. She understood that his behaviors were in response to environmental stressors. Many adopted protocols focus on changing the child's behavior through reward or punishment, without attempting to understand the child's lived experiences. Rasha's personal experience with trauma allowed her to naturally approach Julian with compassion. She focused on finding out why Julian was stressed and figuring out how to reduce his exposure to those stressors. Her acceptance of his reality allowed him to begin to examine and validate his own needs.

Rasha's intrinsic recognition of Julian's trauma, and her understanding of the source of that trauma, is now being validated by researchers who are focusing their work on the needs of neurodivergent people. According to a study headed by Dr. Connor Kerns, at the University of British Columbia, children who are on the autism spectrum may be at an increased risk for encountering childhood trauma (Kerns, Newschaffer, & Berkowitz, 2015). In general, trauma is described as either acute (a one-time event such as an assault), or chronic (which reoccurs over time with incidents such as repeated bullying). Over the course of our lives, most of us have experienced some level of trauma, but it can be more common for people with dis/abilities. Both acute and chronic traumas can lead to long-term impact on the mental, emotional, and physical health of an individual.

Peter Levine has outlined the responses to trauma in these three health domains (Levine, 1997, pp.146–150). In general, some of the emotional symptoms of trauma are:

- anger/reactivity

- irritability

- unresponsiveness/psychological numbing

- anxiety

- depression/existential depression

- burnout/shutdown

- emotional dysregulation/outbursts

- dissociation.

Physical symptoms may manifest as:

- poor concentration/memory

- panic attacks/extreme startle reflexes

- hyperarousal/hypervigilance

- lack of energy

- sleep disturbances/night terrors

- reduced immunity

- flashbacks/shakiness

- increased physical illness

- digestive issues

- autoimmune diseases

- metabolic syndrome.

And behavioral responses can be:

- compulsion

- addictive behaviors/substance abuse

- impulsiveness

- isolation

- lack of motivation

- need to control/rigidity

- hyperactivity/hypervigilance

- difficulty with social demands.

Children are generally more vulnerable to experiencing traumatic events and chronic stressors because they are dependent on adults for their care. Children who are 2eA or autistic may be even more at-risk for victimization and maltreatment, due to communication and social difficulties. In addition, they may be more susceptible to daily stressors that are not a problem for most neurotypical people. These can be experiences such as a noisy classroom, a strong smell in the cafeteria, being bumped while in line, confusing social expectations, or being disciplined for their authentic behaviors (such as stimming or hand flapping). For autistic people, chronic stressors and trauma can put them at significantly higher risk for anxiety and depression.

Yet, many professionals who work with autistic people do not understand this increased risk and may underestimate the impact of daily life on their mental health/stress level. Medical and therapeutic practitioners may misdiagnose behaviors or overlook physical and emotional manifestations of this trauma. Prescribed treatment protocols can further exacerbate the trauma for 2eA people and may inhibit their ability to live a satisfying and productive life. However, there has been a movement toward positive change, as more research is being conducted on meeting the needs of autistic people, and there are many autistic adults who are beginning to advocate for their community (I have tried to mention many of them throughout this book). This activism is building a stronger voice for integration of ideas and actions that respect autistic culture.

ADVICE

The following suggestions are designed to provide parents with ideas for helping their 2eA children, as well as suggestions for young 2eA adults to help themselves.

For Parents of 2eA Children

~ Support 2eA children's deep interests as a crucial part of their developing identity. Helping facilitate the exploration of their passions is very validating and reassuring.

~ Advocate for your child, support them when no one else does. Knowing that your parents are your strongest ally is the greatest protective factor you can provide them.

~ Don't underestimate the levels of trauma 2eA people may be experiencing throughout childhood, particularly at school or in therapies that are based on suppressing or changing innate behaviors.

~ 2eA people are able to see connections and patterns at multiple levels, including the ability to analyze their own thoughts and how they relate to the whole. Your child may continually analyze everything around them; you can support them in creating systems that work for them based on their self-knowledge.

~ Environmental stressors can derail functionality, and 2eA people often need to escape through stimming, dissociating, or literally escaping. Help change their environment to reduce or eliminate those stressors.

~ Going into a stressful environment, such as school or social activities, may require intense mental preparation. Recognize that your child may be gearing up for the onslaught, not just being disagreeable to uncooperative.

~ Boring, mundane tasks such as homework, particularly when there are multiple parts, can feel impossible and overwhelming. Try to find ways to mitigate the difficulties or reduce the amount of homework. Using strategies from knowledgeable professionals like Seth Perler[3] can help.

---

3   https://sethperler.com

~ 2eA people may be easily exhausted by the continual verbal, mental, and physical demands of being at school or work. Even talking about preferred subjects can require a great deal of conscious work, as the back-and-forth nature of conversation, or reading and interpreting nonverbal cues, is very challenging. Be empathetic and give them lots of support, including days off when they feel overwhelmed.

~ Swinging between extremes, or rigidity about a certain perspective, can make it difficult to have discussions or resolve disagreements. Help your children learn perspective-taking and collaborative communication skills in a non-stressful, playful, or fun way.[4]

For Young 2eA Adults

~ Understanding your own patterns of behavior and systems of thought is an essential part of exploring your ability and talent. This awareness will help you craft a life that utilizes your strengths and creates a zone of comfort and security. There are some great YouTube videos by autistic activists (mentioned earlier in 'Being an Advocate') that explore many issues shared by 2eA people. (I am hoping a 2eA person will take on this advocacy and education role for the 2eA community.)

~ Some typical social behaviors, such as lying, manipulating, bullying, or retaliating, are difficult for 2eA people to understand. Your own empathy and sensitivity may cause you to be repelled and distressed by such behaviors and reject people who display these behaviors. Trust your instincts about who might cause you harm.

~ Being blunt and truthful can cause social problems, but so-called "norms," such as white lies or ghosting, may seem unnecessary and destructive to 2eA people. You have the right to be honest, but be aware that how you deliver the message may need to be adjusted

---

4   https://geekandsundry.com/rpg-therapy-for-kids-is-a-real-thing-and-it-works

depending on who you are talking with. Code-switching may be necessary in some environments.[5]

~ 2eA people may have difficulty identifying their emotions, or the emotions of others, so you may misread social interactions and situations. If it is clear that you have misinterpreted another's words or actions, ask them to clarify for you. If you feel comfortable revealing your needs, you can explain why you need additional support around the communication.

~ You may feel you do not belong and find yourself constantly questioning your abilities and interactions. You may be lonely because you do not feel accepted when you are being your authentic self. You can experience dissonance between trying to fit in and staying true to yourself. You may need to code-switch to fit in at certain times (like at work), but try to be true to yourself as much as you can. This will help you find compatible peers and situations that actually work for you.

~ Be proud of your 2eA culture and identity. Activism can be a healing pathway and helps to build pride, acceptance, and understanding for yourself and others.

---

5   Code-switching "refers to any member of a marginalized or underrepresented identity adapting to the dominant environment around them in any context" (Washington-Harmon, 2020).

Asynchronous
at College

F OR MANY 2EA PEOPLE, school is a difficult experience that does
not get much better at the post-secondary level. Higher education does not feel like a viable option for many 2eA people. Even if
they do create a path to college, it can be challenging to meet the
social, academic, and emotional expectations they find there. Many
dis/abilities go undiagnosed throughout 2eA children's lives because they are good at masking or utilizing their intellect to cover
their academic difficulties. They are frequently misunderstood and
rarely receive a truly appropriate education. They are often blamed
for their academic or behavioral failures, even though it is likely
due to lack of appropriate accommodation from the schools. This
may not get better as they work to meet college expectations. As
they mature, they may find themselves struggling with even less
support and understanding from those in positions of authority.
Self-advocacy may be the only way they can find recognition and
support.

Kenny

Self-advocacy comes naturally for Kenny, a proud young Black woman who is also 2eA. She grew up in a family of achievers, people who have worked hard to overcome lack of opportunity and oppression. Her Mom earned a doctorate and has taught at a local college for the past 25 years. Kenny's Dad was a promising young lawyer who was killed in a car accident when she was two years old. Despite loss and hardships, Kenny's Mom has carved out a middle-class life for Kenny and herself. Kenny has a good relationship with her Mom and with her extended family. She benefits from having three aunties who live nearby. Her close-knit family has been a source of strength and comfort for Kenny, and she credits them for much of her success. Her Mom and aunties have always been very proactive in supporting Kenny both at home and school.

As a young African American woman, Kenny's giftedness was not readily identified, a common experience for Black children. She experienced having her behaviors defined as "off-task and disruptive," another form of discrimination experienced disproportionately by both autistic and Black children. Kenny's family understood that they would have to push back against the racism that was deeply embedded in the academic system. They knew they would have to work harder than others to ensure Kenny's school experience was positive and productive.

From when she was very young, Kenny's family taught her to self-advocate. They helped her learn to fail and try again until she succeeded, which built her sense of self-efficacy. They knew these two critical skills are central to facing and overcoming discriminatory hurdles. Kenny remembers her Mom telling her that she would likely have to try harder and keep trying until she figured out how to make it work. "I was so rigid when I was younger. My Mom helped me to let go of perfectionism and learn to solve problems creatively. I have the capacity to see multiple solutions to problems, and, through failure, I learned to find a pathway that worked for me."

Kenny was usually bored in class and struggled to redirect her mind to her assigned work. She wanted to talk about the interesting topics that filled her thoughts. Kenny often got in trouble for disturbing class, as she frequently repeated phrases out loud that were related to her thoughts. Many teachers did not understand that this is a form of verbal stimming, labeled *echolalia*. Kenny was frustrated at the lack of opportunity to state her mind, and by the time she got home from school each day, she was bursting to talk.

While Kenny's Mom sometimes felt exhausted by the constant verbal stream, she understood that Kenny needed this continual mental input. Her Mom and aunties treated Kenny like an intellectual equal and included her in many of their discussions. They respected and validated her ideas but didn't hesitate to challenge her if they felt she was not fully informed on the topic. For example, when Kenny was in fifth grade she came home from a museum field trip and told her Mom that Gaugin's work was genius. Her aunties pointed out that Gaugin had abused and exploited the Polynesian women he featured in his work but invited her to say more about her observations. This type of open debate taught Kenny to consider multiple perspectives, and to adjust her thinking when presented with greater knowledge. Growing up with a free and loving exchange of ideas allowed Kenny to safely develop her identity through recognition of her strengths and understanding of her weaknesses.

Kenny's Mom knew that early identification of her abilities and dis/abilities would provide a critical roadmap of her brain. Through a great deal of investigation, she was able to find a university research program that provided a full neuropsychological evaluation at a reduced cost. This evaluation would have been too costly for her Mom to pay for privately, a common barrier to lower-income families. (In the United States, full neuropsychological evaluations cost thousands of dollars and are not provided by schools or paid for by most medical insurance.) Finding this resource gave Kenny's Mom the information she needed to actively seek out effective support programs for both giftedness and autism.

Kenny's Mom knew she would also face challenges based on race. She was an activist in both the Black and 2eA communities and well informed on issues of justice. Through her Mom's work, Kenny heard stories from 2eA people who had been harmed by both ignorance and willful discrimination. She knows her extended family helped to provide a protective barrier against much of the racism and ableism experienced by many in her community. Kenny's Mom has worked throughout her life to find ways for her to succeed.

While her elementary and middle-school education was not ideal, Kenny is grateful that her Mom was able to secure placement in a progressive high school. Throughout her education, Kenny was easily bored and disengaged if the work felt meaningless. Homework had also been a problem for Kenny, as she didn't need the rote practice to grasp concepts and hated having to do the predictable worksheets. Moving into a high school that offered a strengths-based approach may have made the difference for Kenny's educational success. Her school provided some progressive options, such as allowing students to work at their own pace, even if it radically accelerated the curriculum. They were also allowed to demonstrate mastery and reduce required coursework through testing. They could receive credit for a full semester by passing final exams. Through these mastery exams, students could skip prerequisite courses and move into accelerated classes. This gave students more freedom to design an individual approach to learning in most areas, and teachers could move into the role of mentor and facilitator.

In addition to their high ability being addressed, students also received support in areas of academic weakness. For Kenny, writing is a challenge that requires a reduced workload, adaptive technology (such as speech-to-text apps), and relationships that allow her to feel safe enough to make mistakes. "As a person who can do math and science assignments with ease, having an area where I struggled to keep up was really stressful. I never wanted to do any writing because I know it is my weakness. I needed to trust my teachers before I felt I could show my flaws."

2eA people are often perfectionists who need to feel understood and supported before they can embrace failure. To ensure that appropriate support was given to all students, teachers at Kenny's school were trained in utilizing both a strengths-based approach and a suitable level of accommodation. Kenny could demonstrate her knowledge in self-selected projects that she knew would showcase her abilities and learning. She also knew her teachers would provide support if she began to falter or could not find a suitable way to show her gifts.

As part of their progressive academic curriculum, the school incorporated a community-building program that effectively modeled inclusion and acceptance. Students were divided into cohorts who supported each other and held each other accountable. Kenny loved the stability and predictability this provided. Each cohort also spent their high-school years working on a problem that would directly benefit their community. This allowed students to create a meaningful project they were interested in exploring, while also building connections within their local community.

Students' projects could encompass larger communities and be focused on a particular need or cultural value. Kenny loved her final high-school project, which allowed her to explore the needs of her autistic community, particularly those who were also people of color. "This project provided a chance for me to really understand myself, my culture, and identity in a comprehensive way. This was the beginnings of my activism and set me on a path toward a true vocation." Kenny was inspired by both Black and autistic activists, and devoured books such as *How to Be an Antiracist* by Ibram X. Kendi and *NeuroTribes* by Steve Silberman.

Kenny also faced some of her hardest academic challenges during this time too. Writing had always been difficult, and she avoided writing as much as possible throughout most of her school career. Avoidance of the most difficult academic skills is a common response among 2eA students, due to boredom, anxiety, and poor self-efficacy. This disengagement can range from mild to severe, including full school refusal. If students feel that each school day will be an ongoing exercise in failure, they will not become intrinsically motivated to engage. Teachers who understand the needs of 2eA students can find ways to spark interest and assign appropriate work through connecting the curriculum and assignments to the student's passions.

This is what helped Kenny to stay with writing until she developed mastery. When she started her final high-school project, she was highly motivated to produce something that reflected her vision. Her goal was to create a book of stories based on the lives and work of Black activists through the lens of superheroes. To do the work justice, she saw how important it was to effectively express her ideas in writing.

Kenny spent many afternoons in her school's writing lab working with volunteers and utilizing their support. She learned how to develop methods to break her project down into smaller parts and use backwards planning to figure out what she needed to do to create her envisioned end product. These executive functioning[1] strategies made it feel more manageable. Kenny tried many different ways to take notes and keep records that were critical to the project. She worked harder than she had ever worked on anything that year, but she was excited and motivated to get it done. Through this experience, Kenny was able to put the final polish on years of developing her strengths and mitigating her weaknesses. She could focus on her passions in a way that highlighted and celebrated her own unique journey.

Kenny eventually decided to study law and build a career that would allow her to fight for justice. As a Black woman with a recognized dis/ability, Kenny is uniquely positioned to work for change from inside overlapping groups. She is motivated by the stories of suffering she sees in all of her intersecting communities. Kenny

---

1   Executive function skills incorporate working memory (following rules, putting things in order, remembering details, managing time); self-control (managing distraction, delaying gratification, emotional regulation); and mental flexibility (perspective-taking, trying new things, problem-solving).

remembers watching a TedTalk, "#SayHerName," by Kimberlé Crenshaw, which was a defining moment for her. When she heard the names of murdered Black women spoken aloud, Kenny felt a level of rage that was new to her. She made a commitment to herself that she would find a way to fight against racism and sexism through her work.

The rise in abuse toward people of color and those with dis/ abilities exists at disturbing levels. Kenny knows that being autistic and Black can be lethal in the wrong circumstances. When her Mom talked with her about what to do if she was confronted by police officers, she was told to keep repeating that she is autistic. Given the levels of violence toward dis/abled people by many law enforcement agents, Kenny recognizes there is not a great deal of comfort in that. Kenny wants to be in a position of power to create better circumstances for both of her disenfranchised communities.

Her strengths and experiences will certainly be an asset as she studies law, but Kenny is also aware that her differences may require her to find alternative pathways to end goals. She knows that she can get too animated and intense in conversations, particularly when she is confronted with ignorance. Kenny is aware that her need to correct people is off-putting, but her encyclopedic memory means that she is usually right. Kenny is working on building her communication skills, so social differences don't become a barrier to her intellectual contributions.

She finds it frustrating to have social customs dictate how to demonstrate knowledge and discuss differences. She tends to be dismissive and has a low tolerance for "willful defense of a weak position." Kenny can easily hyper-focus on a problem, which isn't great for cooperative group work, but often means she comes up with novel and creative solutions. She can form mind maps in her head and make connections other people don't see. Kenny can generate a mental system of linking ideas that eventually complete the big picture. It took her a while to realize that not all people think this way.

Kenny is often surprised when fellow students don't remember cases they discussed two years ago and how it relates to what they are currently working on. She believes she will clearly excel in interpreting and applying the law, but struggle with the interactive personal side of her career. Kenny's experiences with meeting the requirements of courses and assignments at university have helped her identify what makes work difficult and what she can do to mitigate the problems. She has also been able to find ways to emphasize her gifts, such as her strong memory and ability to see connections, which helps others to see her value.

She finds it validating to be in law school, as it allows her to finally exercise her intellect to its full capacity in an educational setting. The requirements of law school connect well with Kenny's strengths, particularly her strong memory and analytic ability. She loves the logical process of law and finds the work deeply satisfying. For Kenny, researching, analyzing, strategizing, and interpreting cases is a soothing experience. When she is fully intellectually engaged in this process, she feels like the world makes sense. "It's almost a form of stimming, it allows me to feel totally calm and focused."

While her earlier educational experiences were mostly positive, Kenny doesn't feel she ever had to expend a great deal of mental effort in most of her classes. "My biggest struggle during my undergraduate work was commitment and organization. I wasn't super motivated by mediocre assignments, and that lack of motivation worsened my work habits." Kenny recognizes that being in a university with a robust autism support program was what allowed her to persevere and graduate with a good grade-point average. The program helped her with mitigating her issues around writing and executive functioning, as well as providing caring allies and advocates.

For all people, finding a field of study that follows their strengths and passions is a critical component to success. It increases intrinsic motivation and positive self-efficacy and builds tolerance for doing the more difficult tasks. While most people feel more successful when they have found an area of study that utilizes their best assets, for 2eA people, it might be the critical key to accomplishing their goals. They may not be as adaptable to navigating a course with an incompetent professor or grinding through a boring assignment as their neurotypical peers. No one likes those situations, but most people have enough reserves to get through it; whereas people with dis/abilities are already dealing with layers of difficulty and have more obstacles to overcoming combined stressors.

Many marginalized students find that school is not a safe environment. They experience a greater number of stressors that can create lingering trauma. 2eA children may not receive appropriate academic accommodations or social support from knowledgeable teachers. Frequently, their behaviors are seen as maladaptive or manipulative, rather than an effort to communicate a need. The student's dis/abilities can mask their abilities and prevent appropriate intellectual stimulation. Conversely, their abilities can mask dis/abilities, so teachers never understand how hard the student is working just to appear average. 2eA students may also experience a stronger reaction to environmental stressors, such as crowds and noise levels, which can trigger overstimulation and anxiety.

Flexibility is a skill that may need to be consciously learned through membership of a democratic community. Yet finding a democratic school community is difficult for most members of marginalized communities. They have to work harder for recognition or accommodation and are judged more harshly for deviation from the norm. Most school programs do not allow a great deal of self-directedness, as the focus is on adhering to the curriculum and the teacher's expectations. 2eA children need an opportunity to negotiate with supportive adults about how, when, and what they learn. Feeling heard and understood creates a safe space to learn, which is critical for marginalized students, as learning is a vulnerable act.

Those outside of the 2eA community may not even recognize many of the roadblocks that stand in the way. Sometimes, navigating the interpersonal requirements of group work, scheduling a project to completion, or even just enduring the sensory input of a classroom can feel like an insurmountable hurdle. 2eA people often deal with much higher levels of anxiety and increased sensitivities that can also make life feel overwhelming. Managing a schedule, getting to classes on time, navigating the campus, dealing with crowds and noise levels, or adapting to different environments and expectations can all contribute to lower functionality. Being in a field of study that resonates with your interests and utilizes your strengths can provide an antidote to the disabling aspects of being at a university. It can also be extremely validating to be with people who share your passions. There is an ease that comes from being with mentors and peers who understand you at a deeper level.

It can be difficult to find this level of compatibility with others, particularly in your childhood and teens. Choosing particular fields of study or targeted career choices can help to bring people with similarities together. This can be a rewarding and exciting experience for young 2eA adults, as they can find compatible friends and build validating communities. This may be the first time in their lives where they feel proud to be part of the 2eA culture or comfortable enough to stand up for themselves and their community.

Kenny has been lucky in many ways to discover her passions and strengths over her higher-educational years. It has allowed her to excel in her studies, find compatible friends who appreciate her, and begin to figure out ways to give back to her community. She is forming a relationship and career foundation that can help her to build solid friendships and job opportunities throughout her life. Kenny can embrace her whole self because she is surrounded by like-minded people who share her desire to change the world and understand that we need diversity to make that change.

Reuben

Successfully completing high school can be an unachievable goal for some 2eA students. They may need to create a new path toward earning a college degree. This was the case for Reuben, who dropped out of high school after his first year. His parents were devastated, they felt he had so much potential, but he just couldn't see it for himself. School had always been boring and difficult for Reuben. As early as elementary school, he noticed that things he found hard to do seemed to come easier to others.

He had trouble paying attention in class, and often forgot what he was supposed to be doing. Writing was a struggle, both the ability to string words together and actually putting pencil to paper. Reuben often refused to write because his handwriting looked like a kindergartner's, with large block letters, uneven spacing, and messy formation. He was extremely embarrassed to have anyone see his writing and avoided doing it whenever he could. If forced to write, Reuben tried to find a way to answer the questions with as few words as possible, which resulted in a large disparity between what he knew and what he was able to put in writing.

Reuben had this problem with most of his schoolwork. For example, he was able to read well and knew a lot about many subjects; but he couldn't adequately demonstrate his knowledge, due to his writing issues or because those topics never came up at school. Even in math, a subject he loved, he had difficulty doing the problems he was given. Reuben rebelled by refusing to do most of his work and disengaging in class.

Homework was another area where Reuben rebelled. By middle school he had stopped trying to do any homework assignments. When he was younger, it was a torturous nightly exercise for both him and his Mom. She couldn't understand how someone so smart would find homework such a challenge. He took hours to do one worksheet and was resistant to letting her help. His Mom insisted he could finish it in no time if he just put his mind to it. But Reuben knew he couldn't do it easily, and that made him feel stupid.

He felt like no one understood that anticipating what was coming, and then trying to do the work, took an emotional and intellectual toll on him. His parents often talked with his teachers about how difficult the homework was for Reuben, but his teachers told them that he was a capable student. They felt that he could do better if he just put in more effort, but Reuben knew he was working as hard as he could endure.

He felt there must be something truly wrong with him. In addition to school being a daily struggle, he had difficulty figuring out what people meant or why others seemed not to get what he was trying to say. His Mom often scolded him for being rude and had to regularly remind him to use good manners. Reuben thought people made too big a deal about manners and rudeness. He found it frustrating that people talked in circles and took so long to get to the point of what they wanted from him. Sometimes he just walked away from someone mid-sentence because he couldn't tolerate the length of time it was taking them to explain something.

Reuben also had trouble telling most of his classmates apart, as many of them looked very similar to him. Other students made fun of him or thought he was being a jerk when he said he didn't know who they were. Eventually, he stopped trying to interact with his classmates, and spent a lot of his recess time walking around the playground by himself. During class time, Reuben tried to avoid talking to other kids if he could, and never volunteered to do partner or group work.

He began to withdraw from interaction with his teachers and cared less about trying to please his parents. To avoid feeling excluded by his peers, he sometimes picked fights or bullied others. The more pressure people put on him to conform, the angrier he became. His parents saw him as defiant, his teachers believed he was lazy, and his peers thought he was a loser; a common experience for many 2eA children.

While it was not always obvious to others, Reuben was very creative. He had a knack for engineering and 3D modeling. From a young age he could build amazingly intricate Lego constructions that had delicate moving parts. He was curious about how things worked and liked to take apart old electronic equipment to see what was inside. He checked electronic manuals out of the library and watched YouTube videos about repairing electric household items. He repeatedly asked his parents to buy him a soldering iron and tools and to let him try to repair their broken things. They were concerned that he might electrocute himself, so didn't encourage that pursuit.

Reuben also loved logic puzzles and went through a phase where he built Lego boxes with multiple keys to hidden chambers. He created secret codes and ciphers, and taught himself sign language, Morse code, and nautical signal flags. Much of what Reuben was good at doing did not help him in school. He rarely had a chance to do anything that reflected his strengths or allowed people to understand his intellect. During the school year he came home exhausted most days and felt disconnected from everything he enjoyed.

As a teenager, Reuben began to rebel in earnest. He often refused to go to school, and when he did attend, he frequently cut classes. He never participated in class or did his homework. Reuben got in enough fights to be suspended several times. He failed all of his classes his first year of high school and was assigned to a summer-school program. He refused to participate over the summer and decided to drop out of high school.

Reuben's parents were very upset and tried every parenting technique to convince him to return to school. They bribed, pleaded, and threatened, to no avail. Reuben began to spend a great deal of time in his room. His sleep schedule became irregular and his parents often had to wake him when they got home from work. They didn't know what to do to motivate him, so began to try to find help. They talked with his teachers, the school psychologist, and even tried to hire a tutor, but Reuben refused to participate in anything they offered.

No one seemed to notice that Reuben was burned out, they attributed his behavior to rebellion and defiance. They didn't have any knowledge about twice exceptionality, and their training about autism was basic and standardized. They had no understanding of the needs of 2eA students. Reuben's parents didn't know what to ask to find answers, and the professionals they did consult were not knowledgeable about 2eA either, so did not provide competent advice or care. Since nothing they tried had worked, Reuben's parents were reduced to just hoping that he would eventually get bored and think about going back to school.

But they didn't give up on him, they loved their son and wanted him to be happy and successful someday. They tried to reconnect with Reuben on a personal level and began to invite him to do activities they knew he loved. They gave him space to explore his options and stopped talking about returning to school. Over time, Reuben began to feel less angry about failing school. Not having to attend school, and deal with all the difficulties it entailed, was a huge relief. He was also relieved that his parents seemed to be less focused on school. He could see they were struggling, but felt they were really trying to be supportive. Some days he even woke up feeling happy. His parents began to notice that he was more relaxed and willing to engage in conversations with them. They saw glimmers of his sense of humor again.

Reuben began to feel his energy and curiosity return. He spent many hours watching YouTube how-to videos once again. When he again requested tools, his parents agreed to buy them, partly because he was older, and partly because they were relieved that he was showing interest in something again. Reuben started to fix things at home, and then for his neighbors. Eventually, his reputation grew. He set up a shop in his garage and started a small electronics repair business.

As his ability to fix more and more sophisticated equipment increased, he decided he wanted to specialize in computer repair. When he had exhausted all of the online learning opportunities, he found computer technician classes at his local community college. Reuben signed up for a class without concern for grades or credits, it was the knowledge he was interested in obtaining. He felt this was his first real learning experience. He liked the class, enjoyed his teacher, and even found that his classmates seemed friendly and relaxed.

At the end of his first semester, his professor told him he had a natural talent and should pursue more in-depth classes in computer engineering. Reuben began to think about it but was still worried about enrolling in difficult classes. He didn't want to fail at this too. But as he successfully completed more and more computer technician courses, he began to be intrigued at the idea of a degree in engineering.

Then in a casual conversation with a classmate about how hard it was to do written assignments, he learned about the disabled student services office. Reuben made an appointment to talk with a counselor at his community college. After listening to Reuben's experiences at school, she told him she thought he may have some learning dis/abilities. She recommended that he find someone to do an assessment so they could offer him the appropriate support. When Reuben told his parents about the conversation with the counselor his Mom burst into tears.

She told Reuben that she felt they had failed him. It had never occurred to her that he might have learning dis/abilities because he was so smart. She thought he was being defiant about practicing things like handwriting, or just didn't care about doing his work and getting good grades. Reuben cried too. He told her that he always felt like he was stupid and misunderstood. That conversation was the turning point in his life. Reuben felt like there might actually be a reason why school was so torturous for him. He realized for the first time that it might not have been his fault.

Reuben's parents arranged for a full evaluation with a psychologist. The psychologist referred him to an occupational therapist for further testing. The compiled results showed that Reuben had dysgraphia,[2] autism, and ADHD. When the psychologist explained how this diagnosis could impact learning and schooling, Reuben and his parents felt they finally understood why school had been such a struggle.

Then the psychologist told them that Reuben was also exceptionally gifted, which was a surprise to everyone. His parents had always believed he was smart, but they didn't realize just how high his intelligence was. Reuben was very interested in learning from the psychologist what each of the tests meant and how they were compiled. He felt that he finally had a grasp on how his brain worked and could begin to release the shame he had experienced growing up.

Reuben began to meet regularly with the counselor at the disabled student services office. She helped him figure out his class schedule and what accommodations would be most beneficial for each class before he registered. She recommended that he only take one or two courses per semester, to reduce the workload and help him manage school. He began to feel he had an ally on campus and his confidence grew with each class he completed. Eventually, he began to believe his first professor might have been right in telling him to pursue computer engineering.

When Reuben had completed every computer technician course, he took his first computer engineering course and fell in love. Everything about it made sense to him. He could picture the diagrams in his head and understood intuitively the inner workings of each computer system they studied. "It was like doing the world's best logic puzzle all the time! My brain was finally doing what it was meant to do, and the fog lifted." Reuben excelled in his coursework. Once he had finished every computer course they offered, his counselor encouraged him to begin to take general education classes that would allow him to transfer to a four-year university computer engineering program.

---

2   Dysgraphia: a condition that impacts one's ability to write by hand, due to neurological impact on interactions between the hand and the brain. It can limit ability to form letters and to write quickly by hand. It may also impair spelling ability.

With support from the disabled student services office, Reuben was eventually able to complete coursework and transfer to a university. Through understanding his dis/abilities, finding support networks, and adjusting the pacing of his classes, Reuben succeeded in completing his computer engineering degree. "It took me nine years to finish what other people might do in four, but I got it done. I am working at a job I love, for a company that values me enough to accommodate my issues. I'm surrounded by people who are a lot like me, and that makes me feel successful. When I think about being a high-school dropout, I can't believe where I am now."

ADVICE

Having an awareness of your needs, advocating for accommodations, and working toward your strengths are all key to successfully completing your goals. Following are some suggestions for finding and completing a field of study.

~ If you have limited finances, contact your potential school's financial aid office. They can help you apply for federal grants, as well as alert you to specific scholarships that can cover the costs of many programs. You can also begin your classes at a community college, as they have lower tuition fees than four-year universities. In some states, community college may even be free for students with low socio-economic status.

~ Some states/countries allow enrollment in community college when you turn 18, even if you don't have a high-school diploma. This can be a way into higher education if you were not able to complete high school. Check your local community colleges to see what their policy is on enrollment.

~ Start slow, try taking one class your first semester. For many 2eA people, transitions are difficult, and you may need a little time to feel confident and establish new routines around starting university or college.

~ Start with your strengths. Take that first single class in an area of high interest/high ability. Find one that allows a Pass/Fail grade, or a class that has limited coursework requirements to ease your transition.

~ Analyze your triggers and make adjustments. If you have a panic reaction to being in the middle of a crowd, select a seat by the classroom door. If asking questions publicly creates stress, make arrangements with your professor to email questions after the lecture. If writing notes takes all your concentration and makes you miss too much else in class, record the lecture or see if you can get a notetaker through your disabled student services office. You can find support and allies to help you enjoy your experience and succeed at college.

~ Take advantage of the dis/abled student services at your college/ university. They can be a great asset in helping you to mitigate your dis/abilities. Dis/abled student services personnel can provide accommodations such as distraction-free individual testing areas, extended deadlines, audible textbooks, class notetakers, sensory support, preview of coursework, and extended testing windows. The dis/abled student services staff can be terrific allies in your quest for a degree.

~ Use organizational apps, handwritten lists, or scheduling programs to help you plan ahead in detail. Try to include as much information as you can about assignments, expectations, and events. Having a pretty clear picture of future expectations can help reduce anxiety and rigidity. It can also help you to make alternative plans in case your first plans change, and to anticipate difficulties you might have with what is upcoming.

~ If you haven't already mastered the skill of self-advocacy, work toward being able to state your needs and ask for help. Most people will be supportive and willing to help. If you have registered with the dis/abled student services office, your professors are legally required to accommodate your needs.

~ While you might readily find allies and supporters in higher education, you may need to help them understand the unique needs of a 2eA person. Many do not understand the intersection of giftedness and autism. You may find that they fall back on what they know about autism and/or giftedness, but not truly understand that being 2eA presents its own set of strengths and challenges. For example, they may not understand that you can easily understand and analyze course materials, but have difficulty constructing a product that can demonstrate your knowledge. It may be that you can mentally compute and see the mathematical solution, but struggle to write out the required notations. They may not know that the sensory overstimulation of the lecture hall can make concentrating nearly impossible.

~ If you are a person who has difficulty with conformity or compliance, find a college that allows you to design your own program, or one that doesn't use a formal grading system. Some universities and colleges award degrees based on a portfolio, body of work, or project.

~ You may want to look for universities that have a program designed around the needs of people with autism, such as the Strategic Alternative Learning Techniques (SALT) Center at the University of Arizona or the Boro Autism Support Initiative for Success (BASIS) Program at Edinboro University. There are many alternative programs offered around the world; find one that feels like home to you.

~ If you are not sure how to select a field of study that will direct you to a successful career, consider a major that is of high interest to you. Studying something that you enjoy can be a powerful experience and help to open your mind. There are life skills to be gained just from going to college/university and having new experiences.

~ Having said that, look into what jobs your degree qualifies you to do. Sometimes the area of study is interesting, but the actual job requirements would not suit your abilities. For example, you may be fascinated with studying psychology, but realize you would not enjoy or do well at listening to clients tell you their problems all day long. However, you might be great at conducting psychological evaluations and writing reports, so that could be a viable way to use a psychology degree.

~ Overexcitabilities can be debilitating, but they may also be an integral part of one's identity and potential. Understanding over-excitabilities may be an important step toward building supports and pathways you need to thrive. They might also be the key to your success, as imaginational and intellectual overexcitabilities can be used spectacularly in your career.

~ Sleep is elusive for most college students; but 2eA people may have even more difficulties getting enough sleep. They may not be able to calm their thoughts. Sensual overexcitabilities may also create extreme sensitivity to sounds, light levels, and physical sensations and prevent them from being able to relax into sleep. Using ear plugs, sleep masks, or sound machines, or listening to audiobooks, podcasts, or ASMR,[3] can help to reduce overstimulation and mental clutter.

---

3   Autonomous Sensory Meridian Response, a term for the sensation people get when exposed to certain visual or auditory stimuli that can create a tingling feeling in the back of the head and along the spine. For many, this feeling is deeply relaxing and can help them to fall asleep.

Making It Work at Work

W HILE MOST 2EA PEOPLE have passions that can lead to expertise and deep knowing, they often struggle to translate those skills to the workplace. Even if they have found a field where their skills are highly commercial, other aspects of being 2eA, such as impulsivity, rigidity, perfectionism, or low frustration tolerance, can hijack their success. These stories will cover strategies for finding or creating a way to earn a living.

Jax

Jax is a 28-year-old 2eA entrepreneur. He is tall and thin, attractive by most standards, but unaware and unconcerned about his appearance. He is an introverted person, preferring to spend time alone or with his animals. Jax has not had any close friendships or romantic relationships in his life so far. He has always had difficulty relating to people. He doesn't understand what most people value, as he has never cared about owning things or having status. He also finds social interactions bewildering and exhausting. When more than one person is talking at a time, Jax cannot focus on any conversation. He feels overwhelmed by the sensory input when there are a lot of people around him. Jax was bullied in school, which he believes was because he was socially different and reserved. He remembers wanting to fit in when he was young; but as the years of bullying continued, he withdrew in self-preservation.

When Jax completed high school, he adamantly refused ever to go to school again, despite his parents' long-held expectations. After a year of repeated failures at pressuring him to go to college, his parents gave him an ultimatum: either find a job or go to college. Jax opted to find a job, despite feeling terrified at the prospect. He didn't even know how to begin looking for a job, or what types of jobs he might be qualified to do. Jax's parents helped him look through job postings, fill out applications, and practice what might happen in an interview.

Despite their support, Jax was terrified and ended up having panic attacks that prevented him from even calling to begin the initial application process. Finally, his Dad enrolled him in a local placement service that helped people with dis/abilities find jobs. With their help, Jax was placed at a local chain store as a stock clerk, cleaning and filling shelves. While he was extremely nervous when he started work, Jax was comforted by the knowledge that the job was fairly simple, and the supervisor's expectations were low. He also did not have to interact with the public, as his work was done in the early hours of the morning before the store opened.

Jax was able to work enough hours to satisfy his parents' requirements and, over time, began to feel comfortable on the job. His co-workers were pleasant but didn't make efforts to include him in conversations as they worked. Jax believed that part of the reason for this was his affiliation with the dis/abled person's placement service. His co-workers saw him as dis/abled, and, consequently, lowered their expectations of him. While he found their attitude to be dismissive and ableist, not needing to engage socially at work was a relief for Jax. This helped to lower his stress and allow him to do his job well.

Jax was punctual and followed instructions to the letter, which made his supervisor happy. Since the job didn't really require him to think, Jax was able to keep his mind occupied through listening

to podcasts or music while he worked. He had always been able to hyper-focus on a task and that helped him be good at his job. The minimum wage paycheck was not much, but his parents had not asked him to pay for room and board, so he was able to bank all of his earnings. They encouraged him to save his money for something he might need in the future. He knew his parents were secretly hoping that he would eventually get tired of his job and start college; but Jax knew he was not ever going to fulfill their wish.

Jax worked as a stock clerk for four years before the monotony of his job began to wear on him. By this time, he felt comfortable enough with his work experience to try to find a job that would be a bit more intellectually satisfying. He found work at a veterinarian's office cleaning cages and caring for the animals overnight. Again, he was in an environment that did not require much human interaction. This suited Jax, and he had the added bonus of being around animals.

Jax had loved animals for as long as he could remember. His family had always had family pets, and when he was younger, learning about animals had been one of his main interests. He had an encyclopedic knowledge of animals around the world, including many that most people didn't know existed, such as a fossa, nyala, or gharial. As a young boy, he would often astonish people with this knowledge, casually relaying vast amounts of information about animals and their habits to anyone who would listen.

Once he had learned all there was to know about animals and their habitats, he became interested in animal behavior. He began to study both natural behaviors and those that could be trained. Jax found a great deal of information about how animals have been trained throughout history and what types of behaviors they could be trained to do. He began to work on training their dog to do simple tricks. Then he began training their cat. As his skills at training his pets improved, he began to work on more impressive animal tricks. His animals were the most well trained in the neighborhood.

In his new job, Jax's skill with animals became an asset at work.

He was patient, kind, and good at calming animals. The veterinarian techs noticed his skill with animals and started asking him to walk the most anxious and aggressive dogs before he went home in the morning. Jax began to use his knowledge of animal behavior to help these dogs be more relaxed and confident. He used treats and toys to gain positive attention, and physical touch and ample play to reduce their fear. As his efforts with the animals showed results, he was often commended and felt his skills were appreciated. Jax began to enjoy being around the people at work, almost as much as the animals.

Jax now found it easier to talk with the veterinarian techs when they came in each morning. It was not as difficult as other social interactions, because he knew what they wanted to talk about and what he wanted to tell them. There was no ambiguity in these conversations, so he didn't feel as anxious. He also had confidence in what he was talking about, and the veterinarian techs respected his knowledge and suggestions.

The more he interacted with his co-workers, the more comfortable he became with basic socializing. He found he could ask them how their dog was doing, or if they did something fun on the weekend, without feeling bored or anxious. Over time, Jax began to feel part of a community and found he liked that degree of social connection. After working at the veterinarian's office for over a year, one of his co-workers, Nellie, asked him to train her new puppy. She brought her puppy to Jax's house twice a week, and he trained the puppy and taught her how to continue with the training on her own.

Nellie began to tell people what a great trainer Jax was and, before long, some of the veterinary clients were asking if Jax would help train their dogs. Nellie told Jax that he should start a dog-training business. Jax thought about it; but was worried that he would have to talk to people and wouldn't be very good at that. He continued to work at the veterinarian's office, but occasionally found himself thinking about starting that small business. Nellie continued to encourage him, as some clients were still interested in having him train their dogs.

By now, Jax felt more comfortable with work-related conversations and expectations. He still didn't want to socialize with any of his co-workers, but he enjoyed most of his day-to-day interactions with them. His social circle outside of work continued to be mainly with his parents and extended family. Jax still lived at home, but over the years had created a basement apartment and paid his parents room and board. "I was older and more experienced, so social and work demands did get a bit easier. I did okay at work, but still felt panic at the idea of being an adult on my own."

Jax knew he was capable of working and running his own small household, but old anxieties haunted him. It felt reassuring for him to live in his parents' home, and to have dinner with them regularly. His parents did not pressure him to move out, as they could see he would need a longer time to fully launch into adult life. They were very supportive of him, but still encouraged him to expand his social circle and to start his dog training business.

Because Jax had created a system for living his adult life in a functional and comfortable way, his anxiety levels were lower, and he felt capable and in control. Jax feels that this level of comfort was what eventually gave him the confidence to start his business. He knew his own needs and abilities and felt he could create a business that worked for him. "It helps to be a very systematic person, I read a lot about how to start your own business and then just did it step by step."

Jax began with clients from the veterinary practice and built his business through word-of-mouth recommendations. He struggled with certain aspects of running a business, such as requesting payment for his services, but his skill with the dogs made up for his awkwardness with humans. "I felt that talking about the dogs with their owners gave us a common language. Conversations about training are predictable and in my area of expertise. That framework makes it feel doable."

His reputation and business continued to grow. Eventually, he had to quit his job at the veterinarian's office because he had too many private clients to do both jobs. His reputation for rehabilitating aggressive or traumatized dogs led to his being hired by the County Sheriff's office to work with their police dogs. Jax was able to build a successful dog training and rehabilitation business that allowed him to earn a good income. He has been successful enough to hire a person to work for him part-time and do the public-facing aspects of his business, which allows him to focus fully on the dogs. "It's cool to realize I can make money from something I am naturally good at doing and have been doing since I was a kid. I've found my place in the world."

Jax can deal with the more difficult aspects of his business, like interacting with people or collecting payment, because he is not stressed about the other aspects of his work. He has created a situation where the majority of his day is spent doing something he has a talent for doing and loves to do. Since he is not depleted by the hours he spends with the dogs, he can find reserves to complete the more stressful aspects of his work. Overall, Jax has achieved a balance that is sustainable and supportive of the type of life he wants to live.

Jax had created a successful work niche, but this is not the case for many 2eA people, as those with dis/abilities are disproportionately unemployed. Finding sufficiently paid work to support themselves is often hampered by the employer's lack of understanding or willingness to provide accommodations in the workplace. Typical 2eA traits and behaviors may be seen as an impediment to employment, but these same traits and behaviors can be strengths in an appropriate environment. Financial security may be tenuous for many 2eA people. This is true for Lauren, a talented artist who struggled to earn a living from her artwork.

Lauren

By her mid-20s, Lauren was exhausted. She had worked many odd jobs over the years, from temporary office work to pet sitting. The effort to find and keep jobs took a toll on her well-being. The only place she has ever felt truly at ease is at home in front of her easel. Interacting with the outside world requires a great deal of preparation, both in mobilizing to physically get out the door, and in psyching herself up for the inevitable encounters with others.

Going out has always been a cacophony of sensations for Lauren, as she experiences input at much higher levels than the average person, and in multiple ways. She can see flashes of color when she hears a horn honk or a bird sing. When she is in a crowded space, Lauren often feels as if people have bumped or jostled her, even when they haven't. When she is eating particular foods, she experiences sounds that no one else seems to hear. As a child, Lauren occasionally made a comment about her experiences, but most people just assumed it was her active imagination. When she started school, and realized that others did not share her experiences, she stopped talking about them to anyone.

Lauren learned to cope with these extra sensations by limiting sensory input as much as possible. When she needed to be in a space where she could not control the input, she tried to withdraw into herself or mentally zone out through the worst of it. She became quite proficient at dissociating from her body and her surroundings. While it helped her feel more in control, this dissociation created problems in school. Lauren never felt she was a good student. Many of her report cards noted that she spent too much time "daydreaming" or "needed to pay more attention in class."

The only subject Lauren loved was art, and her talent was evident from an early age. She was encouraged by her parents and teachers to develop this skill and set her sights on applying to an art college one day. But they didn't understand how hard Lauren worked just to be an average student. Once she reached high school and the expectations increased, she struggled to meet deadlines, complete assignments, and pass courses. While the adults in her life offered various types of support, they also contributed to the pressure she felt to succeed. Lauren's grades began to suffer, and she felt like a failure. The pressure from her parents to complete her work made her withdraw further into herself.

Despite increasing anxiety and depression, Lauren continued to try to finish her schoolwork and pass her courses. By her senior year, Lauren was often depressed and barely passing her classes. She began to feel that she could not muster the energy to complete school. She was also very anxious about the expectation to graduate and go to college. She didn't feel she was capable of becoming a functional adult.

Her parents tried to get her to join in activities or call her friends, hoping this would cheer her up. When she did rally to meet or call her friends, afterward she questioned her ability to be a friend and would fall into despair. She became intensely sensitive to others' perceived judgments of her and struggled to make even the most basic decisions. Like many 2eA people, Lauren felt her values and needs did not match those of others in her society. She seemed to experience everything more intensely and struggled to dismiss the cruelty and negativity she saw happening in the world. She felt she had to continually mask her true feelings and experiences to fit in with others.

Lauren ended up withdrawing from her friends and spent all her energy trying to do her schoolwork and avoid disappointing her parents. Given her perceived high-school failures, Lauren couldn't imagine how she would cope with the demands of adult life. She began to experience existential depression and sank into a deep feeling of hopelessness.

After a suicide threat, she was taken by her parents to the emergency room, where a psychiatrist prescribed medication and referred her for follow-up counseling. Lauren started weekly therapy designed to help her work through her depression and self-loathing. Lauren did not fully embrace her therapist's approach to treatment and was uncomfortable telling her therapist about her unusual sensory experiences or her difficulties with fitting into normal life. However, her work with her therapist was helpful in lifting her depression and she began to feel she could once again cope with life. She was able to struggle through her last half of her senior year and earn grades that were just enough to graduate.

The support she received also helped her learn to self-advocate and develop safe, predictable routines. Over time, Lauren began to figure out ways to engage in life while avoiding sensory overload. She altered her sleep schedule to allow her to be awake at night when her parents were asleep. She enjoyed the uninterrupted quiet and solitude that being a night owl provided. Lauren also felt it gave her a sense of autonomy and creative freedom.

Her parents supported her during her first post-high-school year and made few demands on her time. However, as she matured into young adulthood, they began to pressure her to enroll in college. Lauren knew they would not stop trying to control her and was determined to find a way to move out. She took a job cleaning an office building after hours, which gave her a little of the same sense of control she felt being awake at night in her home. Over the next few years, Lauren worked at varying jobs that had a common thread: they were solitary endeavors performed in relatively quiet spaces. She saved her money and looked forward to finding her own place.

Lauren finally found a job she enjoyed, working at an art museum as a night security guard. She appreciated being surrounded by the silent beauty of fine artwork, and the job gave her pockets of quiet time to sketch and read. After nearly two years on the job, she made enough income to rent a small studio space and began to live as an independent adult. Lauren's confidence in her ability to succeed as an adult had grown. She designed a minimalist lifestyle, which suited her, but living on a minimal budget was still hard. She often ate inexpensive, unhealthy foods for weeks at a time to be able to afford art supplies. She went without regular medical or dental care because she couldn't afford to pay insurance premiums. In an effort to help her out, her Mom sometimes procured commissions to create paintings for her parents' friends.

Despite her struggles, Lauren was a good employee. She was frequently commended for her reliability and diligence. Her supervisor occasionally offered her other opportunities at the museum, some that paid a better wage or had more hours, but Lauren always turned them down. She knew that working with the public when the museum was open would be too much for her to handle. To remain in her supervisor's good graces, Lauren felt she needed to make up a plausible reason for staying on the night shift. She worried if she didn't, he might think she lacked ambition or didn't appreciate the opportunities he sent her way. Lauren finally decided to tell him that she attended university classes during the day so could only work at night.

Eventually, Lauren was promoted to the full-time night security guard position, which came with a raise and health benefits. Lauren felt this gave her more financial security and income to take better care of herself. She began to feel confident that she could build a manageable life. She became a more regular customer at her local art store, and sometimes felt comfortable talking with other artists she saw there. She even accepted an invitation to join a group of artists that got together once a week to sketch and critique each other's work. Lauren's life was beginning to take shape, but then she got sick.

Lauren started to experience abdominal pain and fatigue; some days were so bad she could not go to work. She had always had issues with her digestion, so she was not initially alarmed at the bloating and diarrhea she was experiencing. But as the pain and fatigue worsened, Lauren made an appointment to see a doctor. She was nervous about what she would experience at the doctor's office, but more afraid of not finding out what might be wrong.

Fortunately for Lauren, her insurance covered appointments at a renowned university hospital, noted for its research and skilled practitioners. Lauren also lucked into finding a physician who was curious, compassionate, and thorough. After an intake examination, the doctor began to evaluate Lauren's health holistically. She explored Lauren's past physical and mental health stressors and her current daily routines around food, exercise, and sleep. Through their conversations, the doctor began to suspect that Lauren might be autistic and recommended scheduling a neuropsychological evaluation.

Lauren learned that she had sensory-processing disorder (SPD), generalized anxiety disorder, and autism. She was also surprised to learn that she had synesthesia,[1] a condition she had never heard of until then. In talking with the neuropsychologist about her diagnoses, Lauren felt a new level of clarity. All her overwhelming experiences, self-prescribed limitations, and feelings of incompatibility with life now made sense. Lauren was flooded with relief. "For the first time in my life, I thought maybe I wasn't crazy. There were names for what I went through and it's a relief to know there are other people who have the same experiences."

Lauren's doctor knew about the links between autism and gut health, and the impact of sensory issues on immunity and resilience. She diagnosed Lauren with irritable bowel syndrome (IBS) and began treatment that would allow her gut to rest and heal. Unfortunately, Lauren's illness made her miss so much work that she was laid off from her job. The stress of losing her job, and her medical coverage for treatment, increased her symptoms and Lauren became sicker and less able to function.

Lauren's parents were very worried and insisted she move back to their home so they could help her recover. Lauren was shaken by

---

1   Synesthesia: a neurological experience where the senses are blended. Stimulation of one of the senses produces a simultaneous reaction in another. For example, synesthetes may taste colors, hear shapes, or feel sounds. They may experience consistent blended sensory events, such as certain numbers are always the same color, or certain sounds always have the same smell.

her loss of independence and the thought of moving back home in her late 20s but didn't see any other option if she were to survive. Her parents hired a mover to clear out her apartment and put her belongings in storage. They brought all her personal items and art supplies home, but Lauren felt too sick to paint.

She worried about the loss of her medical coverage and didn't want to be a financial burden to her parents. Her Dad helped her apply for state dis/ability insurance, and with the documentation from her former physician, she was able to qualify. The insurance gave Lauren a small monthly stipend and medical benefits provided by the state.

Lauren felt defeated. She was grateful for her parents' support and care, but also depressed by her loss of independence and health. "I felt like I had come full circle, but not in a good way. I figured that I might have to move back home to help my parents someday. I didn't expect that I would become frail! Or they would be the ones who had to help me."

Her parents did help her in many ways. They had both retired in recent years, so were able to provide daily care. They also began to research IBS, studying diets and supplements that others found could help with healing. Lauren's parents also educated themselves about autism, SPD, and synesthesia. They began to understand how the world, and their own expectations, had impacted Lauren's mind and body. Lauren could see the change in how they thought about her, and she basked in their more empathetic approach. She began to feel closer to her parents and to enjoy their company.

As Lauren rested and healed at home, she began to feel hopeful. Then she got a call from her former doctor inviting her to participate in a study on autism and gut health at the research hospital. This study would cover all of her treatment and include care from experts in multiple disciplines, from gastroenterologists to psychiatrists. Participants would meet for weekly group therapy, cooking classes, and outings together, and would take classes to learn about how their minds and bodies were an interconnected system. Lauren was both excited and nervous but signed up for the study. The weekly program included meeting with a psychiatrist who specialized in autism. Through her individual and group therapy, Lauren learned a great deal about her neurobiology. "I was with people who shared my experiences. In the program we learned how life had impacted our health. For the first time, I felt normal, and whole, and part of a community."

Lauren began to regain her health, and a new outlook on life. During her participation in the study, she had many conversations with her parents about what she was learning and experiencing. As they learned more from the research study, her parents were remorseful that they hadn't really understood Lauren's needs and struggles when she was growing up. But Lauren didn't blame them for anything; she understood that they had done what they thought they should do. She was happy that they were growing together as a family and contributing to the greater body of knowledge in ways that might help others like her. Lauren was motivated to change the outcome for girls and women in the 2eA community.

Like Lauren, many 2eA girls are not identified when they are children. They may be good at masking their struggles and often try to blend in at school. Often, their more debilitating experiences are not linked to their behaviors, so may go untreated for much of their lives. They may see themselves as failing to measure up to typical standards and incapable of living a "normal" life. 2eA people are often their own harshest critics and will blame themselves for failing, rather than crediting their efforts or recognizing how much harder they have to work at life. The corrosive impact of chronic stress is well documented in general, but we are beginning to have a better understanding of how stress impacts 2eA people in particular.

Lauren has experienced both mental and physical health conditions due to chronic stress, which was exacerbated by lack of understanding and appropriate support. Early diagnosis and intervention at school could have altered Lauren's outcome. She may have been able to be more successful at school and fully utilize her talent to create a career she loved. Appropriate recognition and support by medical and therapeutic professionals might have intervened in ways that helped Lauren recognize and address her challenges without self-blame. Better understanding of how to parent a 2eA child could have helped her family foster a closer relationship and create a safer environment to explore abilities and develop coping skills.

Many parents of 2eA children have a great deal of love, and desire to provide a stable home, but may not actually know what to do when typical parenting doesn't work. Professionals such as teachers, doctors, and employers often want to provide an inclusive, supportive environment, but might not understand what is needed. If we can build common knowledge about the needs and abilities of 2eA people into our culture, we will be more able to incorporate support structures into society in general.

Lauren's story has a happy ending. Once she recovered her health, she was motivated to live her life to the fullest. She wanted to find a way to make a living as an artist. Through a friend she met in the research group, she found an art degree program with a focus on conservation and restoration. Lauren stayed with her parents throughout her degree program, and their support allowed her to overcome the difficulties of being back in school. When she graduated, Lauren was rehired at the art museum as an apprentice conservation technician and began to learn how to care for the museum's paintings. She rebuilt her independent life; but this time around, she felt she was truly living.

ADVICE

Following are some ideas for creating an achievable, sustainable, and perhaps enjoyable work life.

~ If you are college/university bound, consider fields of study that will result in a career that can be made to fit your social, physical, emotional, and intellectual needs. If you love science and are a night owl, consider an occupation that allows you to work from home or be in the lab on an overnight shift. Or perhaps you love nature and have strong math skills; look into careers that allow solitary fieldwork, such as cartography or geology. Find a pathway that will accentuate your talents, while still allowing you to be your authentic self. A strengths-based approach doesn't disregard your dis/abilities or challenges, but it will give you a way to excel and feel confident. This positive self-efficacy and performance can be a mitigating factor for your challenges. Supervisors are more likely to make accommodations for an employee who is contributing value to the workplace.

~ If you prefer to find a career without attending college/university, start with looking at possible options in books or online, such as *300 Best Jobs Without a Four-Year Degree* by Michael Farr and Laurence Shatkin, or *Better Than College: How to Build a Successful Life Without a Four-Year Degree* by Blake Boles. You might be surprised to discover that people get paid well to do all sorts of jobs that don't require a degree, such as technical writer, bookkeeper, web developer, or professional organizer.

~ Consider apprenticeships and on-the-job training if college/university doesn't feel like it will meet your needs or interests. There are many excellent careers in the trades and para-professional fields. The key is to find something that matches your interests and talents or has the potential to grow your inherent skills.

~ People may judge your career/job choice because they believe you should capitalize on your giftedness and pressure you toward a particular field of study. You should follow your own interests and trust your instincts to do what you want to do for work.

~ Volunteering is an excellent way to build both job skills and resumes. There are opportunities to volunteer in nearly every area of interest. Some of them even provide room and board, such as WWOOF[2] or HelpX,[3] two organizations that allow you to find temporary work in various settings around the world. Volunteering can be a lower-pressure way to build your on-the-job skills and explore possible careers.

~ Be open to considering any possibility that comes your way. There are skills to be learned in any situation and even the most menial job could be a pathway toward other opportunities that match what you really want to do.

~ Working for a temporary agency can be one way to earn an income without undue performance pressure. If you are able to travel to various job sites and don't mind continually interacting with new people, temping can be another way to try out various jobs and companies.

~ Investigate types of work and companies to see if they feel like a good fit for your skills and needs. Research what any particular job entails. Write out your questions to ask at the interview to find out what the environment, expectations, and people are like at your potential workplace. Don't hesitate to bring your notes, or to take notes during the interview, if you need to use them to organize your thoughts and help lessen your anxiety.

~ Many 2eA people have imposter syndrome[4] on the job because a

---

2   https://wwoof.net
3   www.helpx.net
4   A term used to define a habit of doubting your abilities and feeling like a fraud. It disproportionately affects gifted people, because they often have difficulties seeing their level of accomplishment.

2eA brain may be wired to be a specialist rather than a generalist. Many jobs don't include a description of everything that could be expected of you at work. 2eA people can feel blind-sided when they are asked to do something that was not in their original description of the job. Coupled with the common trait of perfectionism, many 2eA people feel they are failing when the task set is too broad. Try to find jobs where you are not expected to be a generalist but allowed to focus your energies on those things you are best at doing.

~ Some of the common workplace norms such as "fail fast"[5] or open plan offices can be a nightmare for 2eA people. Investigating the work environment can help you either advocate for a more friendly option or look for an alternative workplace.

~ Try to create a work–life balance that feels right to you. Most 2eA people need downtime to recharge, as work requirements and expectations can be very exhausting. Non-2eA people don't always understand how much energy 2eA people might be expending just to function at a baseline level in certain aspects of their jobs. For some, the social aspects are difficult; for others it is the executive functioning tasks, such as being on time or adhering to schedules. Make sure your supervisor understands both your abilities and dis/abilities, and ask for help when needed.

~ That is not to say that every supervisor will be supportive, despite legal mandates to do so. Some people are ignorant and biased, so you may find that you are in a work environment that is too oppressive to endure. If you feel you are being discriminated against and want to fight it, consult an attorney (there are many organizations that provide free or low-cost legal aid if needed[6]).

---

5   A practice where people try multiple small experiments in a short amount of time to test an idea. It is designed to rapidly find out which ideas will work, and which will fail. It is often used by entrepreneurs in the startup process. It requires a high sense of self-efficacy and ability to transition quickly from one approach to another.

6   For example, The International Legal Foundation: www.theilf.org

If you don't want to fight it, find a sympathetic person who can write a letter of recommendation before you resign. Unfortunately, even an unfair criticism of your work can impede your efforts to find another job. This can be very triggering for 2eA people, as most have a finely honed sense of justice and expect fairness and honesty from others.

~ Be aware of your 2eA traits that might cause problems at work, such as: sensory issues (typically the office lighting or strong scents, but can also include problems like not being aware if you are too hot, too cold, or hungry); executive functioning problems (typically organizational skills and time management, but could include hyper-focus, unawareness of surroundings, and attentional issues); anxiety-related issues (which can include exhaustion from hypervigilance and panic attacks); and boredom (many 2eA people need appropriate intellectual stimulation to stay focused and motivated on the job).

~ Learn all you can about being 2eA. Assess and address your dis/abilities. What do you need to accommodate or resolve to be able to follow through with tasks and expectations? Try to approach tackling your roadblocks in small, manageable chunks. Even if you only work on a problem for a few minutes a day, you are still working on the problem.

~ Trust that you are the expert on yourself. Others may confidently tell you that they know what you need to do to be successful, but you should only follow advice or adopt changes that feel authentic to you.

~ Your mental abilities might operate at a much faster speed than others, so you may need to give them time to catch up to your thoughts and ideas. 2eA people can see connections that make them good at predicting patterns, but others may not be able to follow your thought process. You may need to explain things to others that appear obvious to you.

~ Many 2eA people are hardwired to do deep dives in researching their areas of interest. Make sure the time you spend doing a particular task at work matches what you were expected to do. Don't do more work on a particular project than is needed.

~ The social aspect of work can also be difficult for 2eA people, as many are not aware of how their actions are perceived by others. It can help to work on more nuanced social behaviors, like acquiring diplomacy (for example, refraining from correcting others' mistakes when help was not solicited), or learning how to protect yourself from being manipulated (2eA people can be too trusting and willing to please, and may even be socially gullible, which can make them vulnerable). It can help to find a trusted ally at work, someone to guide you as you learn to emulate office norms; but some 2eA people are observant enough to watch and learn on their own.

~ Search out mentors and allies who can support your plans. In the workforce, you may find programs designed to offer support, such as Specialisterne[7] or Hire Autism.[8] Or look for companies that are actively trying to create autism-friendly environments (such as Ernst and Young, an international accounting firm; Microsoft; AMC Theaters; SAP Softway; and Ford Motor Company).

~ Look into starting your own business. For many 2eA people, being an entrepreneur can be very satisfying and rewarding. Finding an untapped niche that matches your strengths and interests or solves problems that have not previously been addressed is likely to result in success. 2eA adults tend to be good at looking at things from a different perspective, often seeing potential problems before they happen, creating alternative solutions, or even noticing patterns and trends before others do. This is where your intellect, creativity, and quirkiness can give you an advantage, as 2eA people tend to

---

7   https://specialisterne.com
8   https://hireautism.org

have naturally entrepreneurial minds. Temple Grandin's ground-breaking work with animal behavior has famously personified these traits.

~ Remember that no one is smart and capable all the time. We all have times when we fail, so use that to your advantage. Try to build positive self-efficacy around failure to see it as a learning opportunity and pick yourself up to try again.

~ Take care of your mental and emotional health. Recognize that your reactions to life might be more intense and existential than the norm. Being forced to adhere to a more typical value system (like school or work) can create a sense of crisis. It can help to find ways to be your authentic self and openly advocate for a more meaningful life. Seek out a community of equally deep-thinking peers and find support and comfort in knowing you can make an impact on the world in meaningful ways.

Homekeeping

BEING 2EA MIGHT MEAN you have executive functioning deficits, anxiety, sensory-processing issues, fine/gross motor skills difficulties, or attention problems. None of these things makes taking care of yourself and your home an easy thing to do. Imagine not being able to stand the smell of cooking, or the sound of a vacuum cleaner? What if the choices in the grocery aisle feel overwhelming, or having to talk to the clerk is too frightening? Living on your own as an independent adult, with all of its freedom and responsibility, can make 2eA people feel their "gifts" are less than ideal. But there are strategies you can develop that make homekeeping manageable and may even allow you to make your home a safe and inviting place to rest and recharge.

Ronan

Ronan is a transgender man who is also 2eA. He has had a difficult time with finding a place to call home. His parents are strict followers of a conservative religion and kicked him out at age 17 when they learned he was trans. Ronan couch-surfed with various friends' families, relying on their goodwill to help him survive until he could graduate from high school. Once he graduated, Ronan hitchhiked up the coast to an area where he knew an established

LGBTQ community thrived. He found temporary living space through a program that helped homeless LGBTQ youth transition from high school to employment. Through their mental health services, Ronan learned he was autistic and gifted, which he felt explained a lot about why his childhood had been so difficult.

This program also provided an onsite counselor to oversee the daily living tasks, coordinate responsibilities, and facilitate interviews and job placement. This was helpful for Ronan, as he knew how to do basic chores but had never been fully responsible for taking care of his own place. He was grateful for this placement and worked hard to do his fair share and be a good roommate. Ronan was well liked, but, over time, he found group living to be stressful. He struggled to cope with the sensory input, constant social demands, and unpredictability that came with having multiple roommates. Ronan loves quiet and order, and feels he needs downtime to be able to function well in his day-to-day life. He was conflicted though. He wanted to find a place of his own where he had relief from the stress of group living; but was anxious about accomplishing all the aspects of adult living that come with being on your own.

Through the help of his program, Ronan was able to find a job at a local plant nursery. His duties were focused on watering and caring for the plants, as well as helping customers carry purchases to their cars. Ronan found that he enjoyed the peaceful environment, as there were many parts of his job where he worked in quiet spaces. Over time, the nursery owner, Jane, taught him how to propagate, prune, and treat various plant diseases and pests.

Ronan spent most of his free time reading about horticulture and botany, and it became his new passion. Jane appreciated Ronan's interest and willingness to learn and gave him increasing responsibility at the nursery. His naturally kind and sensitive disposition was an asset in getting along with others, both customers and fellow employees. Jane's mentorship gave Ronan a glimpse of his potential and a growing sense of stability. Eventually, the combination of feeling safe at work and longing for a quiet space spurred Ronan to overcome his anxiety and begin looking for a place of his own.

Ronan was fortunate to work in an area that bordered both neighborhoods and rural farmlands, so rents were reasonable. One day, Jane told him about some customers of hers who had recently finished renovating an old farmhouse and were moving out of the caravan they had lived in during the renovation. They were looking for a compatible tenant for the caravan, and their farm was within cycling distance of the nursery. Jane offered to make an introduction, and that was the impetus Ronan needed to meet the owners and see the rental.

While the caravan was old and small, it was clean and well kept. Ronan felt it could be perfect for him. It had one small bedroom and bathroom, a compact kitchen, and combined living/dining area. Most importantly, the owners were willing to rent to him and it was within his budget. The bonus for Ronan was that it was mostly furnished. Ronan loved that the caravan sat under a stand of trees away from the farmhouse and barns. He was longing for a place that could provide respite at the end of each day and was excited at the thought of having his own home.

As Ronan only owned a small number of possessions, he was able to arrange to have one of his former roommates drive him and his belongings to his new home. After they drove away, Ronan began to organize his belongings and look through his new home; opening cupboards, lying on the bed, and sitting at the little table. He found that his landlords, Mike and Cindy, had left him dishes and cooking implements, but he realized that there were things he didn't think about before he moved, like needing bedding, towels, and toilet paper.

He began to feel anxious about what he would need to take care of his home, how he would shop for food, and what else he may have overlooked. Ronan began to pace around his new home and worry that he may have taken on more than he could handle. Just when panic began to set in, he heard a knock at the door. Cindy stood on the porch with a sleeping bag, a loaf of bread, and some eggs from their chickens. When she saw how shocked he was at her offering, Cindy laughed and said that people in this area looked out for each other. Ronan felt some of the tension leave his body and told Cindy he was very grateful for her help.

After Cindy left, Ronan ate some of the bread, read a book, and went to bed. The next day, as he rode his bike to work, he decided to only worry about one problem at a time, starting with the most pressing needs. He asked Jane if he could have two of the plastic crates they used at the nursery to rig onto his bike so he could haul groceries home. After work he went to the local grocery store to see what he could buy to stock his fridge and cupboards.

Ronan has always had difficulty with feeling overwhelmed by choices, so shopping for food was not an easy task. As he began to go through his list of items, the number of choices on the shelves made him feel paralyzed. He wasn't sure which were the best bargains or how to decide which brand he should buy. Ronan was also worried about finding the foods that he knew he liked, and if he couldn't find them, whether another variety might be palatable. He was only able to find and buy about half the items on his list, but he felt he at least had enough food and supplies to get him through the next few days. As he rode home, he decided to try to focus on one day at a time so he wouldn't feel overwhelmed. He knew he would have to make adjustments and learn by trial and error but vowed to be patient with himself.

Ronan began to devise a system to learn life skills. He has always loved to categorize and organize things. As a small child his favorite activity was to arrange his toys by type, shape, or color. As he grew, this talent became evident in the way he researched topics of interest and stored knowledge in his mind. Ronan decided to apply those skills to figuring out what he needed to learn to be independent. He separated the tasks into several categories: cleaning, shopping, cooking, laundry, and finances.

Ronan decided to start with the areas he felt were most achievable. For example, he knew he could eat reasonably well without learning to cook, so he bought items he was already comfortable with eating and didn't require cooking skills. He filled his fridge and pantry with items like granola bars, yogurt, fruit, sandwich ingredients, cereal, and a few microwavable dinners. Ronan knew that cooking would take time to master, but he also thought he could make his food budget stretch and improve his diet if he could prepare his own meals.

As an adult, Ronan is both relieved about having the choice of eating what he likes, and worried about making sure he eats healthily. He has been researching the aspects of a healthy diet and is cautiously trying various foods that will meet those needs. He created a weekly grocery list of his known comfort foods, what he can substitute if they are not in stock, and a weekly new food to try. He has also taken time to walk through the grocery store and make a floor plan of what items are on each aisle, so he does not feel as overwhelmed by the large volume of items and size of the store. Ronan has developed routines that are helping him to feel more in control of food purchasing and preparation.

As summer wore on, Cindy and Mike often left a few items from their garden on his porch. Ronan was motivated to use the produce and decided to try to learn a simple basic cooking technique every week. He also thought this might help him to be able to expand the types of foods he felt he could eat. Food had been problematic for Ronan for most of his life. When he was young, he would only eat a limited number of foods, despite his Mom's effort to get him to eat what she cooked for the family. He struggled with sensory issues around smell, taste, and texture, and could not endure many types of foods. Looking at food as something he can control and enjoy is a new experience for Ronan, but one he is finally beginning to master.

Ronan's next area on his list was cleaning and housekeeping. He is sensitive to the smells of most cleaning products and wanted to find ways to clean his kitchen, floors, and bathroom in a tolerable way. Cindy has been a big help to Ronan in this area, as she is environmentally conscientious and happy to reduce toxins whenever she can. She has taught Ronan how to use baking soda, lemon, salt, and vinegar as cleaning products, all smells that he can tolerate.

The caravan has linoleum floors, so Ronan is able to use a broom to sweep before he mops. He is happy his home does not have wall-to-wall carpet, as the sound of vacuum cleaners has always stressed him out. Since there is no washer/dryer in the caravan, and the nearest laundromat is several miles away, Cindy has also offered Ronan a work-trade option. He helps with farm chores for two hours every week in exchange for using their laundry facilities. There are certain farm chores that Ronan can't do, such as cleaning the chicken coop or animal stalls, due to his sensory issues and anxiety around feces. Cindy was understanding and offered a job that is within his comfort zone, helping with the garden. Ronan is learning many skills from Cindy and feeling more confident about his ability to care for his home.

Ronan is also learning to manage his finances and plan for his future. This is the first time he has had to pay rent, buy his own food, and pay for utilities on his own. Money has not been a driving factor in Ronan's life. He has never been a person who wants to own much, as he feels the world is too focused on consumerism. While Ronan enjoys a simple life that is filled with quietude and is close to nature, he also knows that he will always need a steady, reliable income.

He is continuing to learn more about plants and gardening, and has grown his expertise around organic, sustainable methods. Ronan has even begun to share what he is learning about sustainable permaculture gardening with Cindy and Mike. Jane has encouraged him to take some landscape design classes at the local community college, as she believes he could eventually build a business around designing and building permaculture gardens.

Ronan can picture a pathway to financial freedom through a

career built around gardening. He knows that his simple needs have allowed him to live on a smaller income, but Ronan would like to purchase a laptop and have wi-fi installed at his home so he can take online classes. He is beginning to feel his way into adulthood and, as he becomes more skilled and knowledgeable, he thinks he might even be able to start his own business. Ronan understands that he has a lot to learn about creating a business, and that there might be aspects that would be hard for him.

He has seen how Jane interacts with customers and the clever ways she builds a devoted clientele through monthly social events and her quirky plant catalogues. He realizes that he would need to learn to drive and own a vehicle to run a gardening business; but he also knows there is no pressure to do so. He enjoys working for Jane and knows she is happy with his work, which frees him to daydream about what he might do someday.

Ronan is using his organizational skills to create a budget that allows him to save for immediate needs, like the laptop, through carefully monitoring his other expenditures. He is also thinking about possibilities and planning for his future in a mindful way. He can manage the day-to-day stress because he has designed systems for each aspect of his life. He prioritized the areas that need his attention and focused his efforts tackling them one at a time. Ronan has plans for the future, but knows he can take it step by step, and that puts less pressure on him.

Now in his mid-20s, Ronan's interests, determination, skills, and intellect have helped him to create a satisfying adult life. He acknowledges that he has been helped by friends and mentors, particularly when he was starting out and most in need. He feels that having his own home has given him a stable base to grow his life in many directions. Most satisfying for Ronan is the feeling of peace that comes from the well-organized life he has designed for himself. He has found ways to mitigate the aspects of life that trigger his anxiety and sensory overload.

He is also hopeful for the future, as he believes he can continue to design his life as his spheres of influence and connection continue to grow. Ronan also feels he is part of a bigger community of people who care about nature and the planet. He is confident he will continue to meet kindred spirits, who share his beliefs and passions, and accept him as he is. "My adult life is so much better than my life growing up. I spent my whole childhood being treated as if my behaviors were something to be fixed. I wish I had been a rebellious kid, but I have never been a fighter." Ronan said he probably would have lived at home a lot longer in different circumstances, because change is hard for him. But he is happy that he found the courage to stand up for his true self, as that was the catalyst to the life he has now.

Tahnee

Tahnee doesn't remember feeling different when she was growing up. Her family were free-thinking people who lived an alternative lifestyle in their converted school bus home. She remembers feeling like every day was an adventure, as they lived in a forest. She spent her time playing in the woods and exploring their property. Tahnee's parents believed in unschooling their children, and she had the freedom to determine her own educational path.

She loved nature, animals, reading, writing, and mythology. Tahnee spent her days reading, exploring the natural wonders around her, and writing stories about what she saw. She liked to draw little illustrations in the margins of her stories and sometimes made up fantasy characters and worlds based on what she saw in nature. Tahnee was creative and observant, and her stories and illustrations were rich with the details of what she knew about her forest home and its inhabitants. By the time she was 12, her writing and drawing had reached a level of sophistication that rivaled early Audubon Society texts.

This skill development and attention to detail came from the hours she spent at her work, which was what her parents had envisioned for their children. Her family did not believe in technology. There were no laptops, tablets, or cell phones in their home. Tahnee's Mom believed children should learn through real-world experiences, so she took time to teach them practical skills. Their family values reflected a love of nature and sustainability. Tahnee grew up learning how to live without modern conveniences.

Tahnee's parents had been highly successful corporate executives but opted out of that lifestyle. They decided to leave their urban life and purchased several hundred acres of pristine forest and a biodiesel bus. They had saved enough money to retire early and live a simple life of farming and self-sufficiency. Over the years, they learned how to grow food and care for animals. Their bus home slowly became surrounded by a barn, chicken coop, workshop, and root cellar. As their children came along, they added to the bus until it became the central part of a larger home. Tahnee loved the eclectic feel of her home, with all its odd nooks and interestingly shaped rooms radiating outward from the bus.

They valued craftsmanship and their home was filled with places to create art, build projects, read, and relax. In the winter, they often sat around their large table and worked on individual projects. Tahnee's parents were good cooks and their house usually smelled delicious and inviting. Their children learned to grow and preserve food, treat minor ailments with natural medicine, and repair and maintain their property. Tahnee didn't feel as if she had missed out on any aspect of childhood growing up. Her friends were her younger siblings and her pets. She found entertainment in her daily activities and rarely thought about the outside world. They made or grew most of what they needed and tried to reduce waste wherever they could. Their lives revolved around the ongoing tasks of growing and preserving food and caring for their animals, buildings, and equipment.

Despite the need for daily labor, they also had a lot of time for fun and connection, especially during the winter when farm chores were less arduous. Tahnee's parents taught their children to create things from scratch, like whittling spoons or making paper. Her family spent many enjoyable hours playing, reading, talking, and creating.

Her only real exposure to life outside their property came when her Dad's parents visited. They seemed to marvel at the life their son had created but were somewhat baffled about why they chose to live that way. They loved their grandchildren, and Tahnee loved them. Her Mom's parents had died before Tahnee was born, so she felt grateful for having her paternal grandparents as part of her life. She had many happy memories of reading her stories to her grandma and grandpa or walking with them in the woods to show them her favorite spots. They often told her that she was a very intelligent and talented girl.

When Tahnee reached her teens, her grandparents began to invite her to come to stay for a visit. Initially her parents resisted, as they knew Tahnee was a sensitive child, had never been away from home, and hadn't been exposed to the busy outside world. But Tahnee was curious about her grandparents' home and eager to have them all to herself. Tahnee and her grandparents continued to ask her parents and they eventually relented. Tahnee was very excited to see what life would be like at her grandparents' house. They arranged to have her spend Christmas with them at their home in the suburbs.

As they drove to her grandparents' house, she marveled at how many cars, buildings, and people were around her. Once they arrived, Tahnee was surprised to find how large her grandparents' house was. The vaulted ceilings and clean furnishings seemed quite empty compared to her small cluttered home. But her bedroom was comfortable, and she was happy to crawl into bed after her long trip. The next morning, she was surprised to wake to a variety of low-level noise. She could hear traffic and neighbors outside, the sound of a TV, the hiss of an espresso machine, electronic beeps from a microwave, and the whir of a blender.

Tahnee found herself tensing up with each sound. She jumped when her grandpa knocked on her door and told her to come to breakfast. Her grandparents wanted her visit to be fun, so they took her sightseeing, shopping, and to some holiday events. Throughout her stay, Tahnee was not able to adjust to the noise levels. It made her feel edgy and uncomfortable. She also had trouble paying attention to her grandparents' questions and comments, particularly if they were in a crowded public place. By the end of each day, Tahnee was exhausted and couldn't wait to go to bed.

Her grandparents began to worry about her health and lack of energy. Her grandma asked her questions about how she was feeling and tried to determine what might be causing her lack of enthusiasm. After a few nights of turning down invitations to go to a movie, or walk through the town to look at lights, her grandparents called their son and daughter-in-law. They reminded them that she was a highly sensitive child, and this was all new to her. Her parents suggested they give her a few more days to adjust.

They also thought she might be homesick, since her first solo trip was into a very different environment. Tahnee made it through the entire week of her visit, but she was emotional and couldn't explain why she was feeling so uncomfortable. When she returned home, her parents attributed it to homesickness. Since she seemed to bounce back quickly, they didn't concern themselves about it further.

Tahnee wondered if there might be something more to it because she felt so much different at home. She immediately noticed how quiet her surroundings were compared to her grandparents' house. She also noticed how peaceful and relaxed she felt, and how much more energy she seemed to have. Tahnee kept thinking about the difference and wondering why sounds had so much effect on her. She started to take note of when she felt the most at ease and found that it corresponded to when it was quiet. When she was walking in the woods, or in the barn at night with the animals, or even falling asleep in her bed, she noted that those gentle, natural sounds did not upset her.

She also felt as if she were physically connected to the forest. When she walked in the woods Tahnee could almost visualize her body absorbing the molecules around her. Any time she was angry or sad, walking in the forest would immediately change her mood. Tahnee was grateful that she had been raised in such a peaceful place and that her parents had chosen a simple, old-fashioned life.

However, as she grew older, she became more interested in the convenience and technology of her grandparents' world. Over the next few years she visited her grandparents more often and found that she could tolerate the noise and bustle a little better over time. Her grandmother had also done some research on why Tahnee was so sensitive to sound and told her what she had learned about sensory-processing disorder and highly sensitive people. With that initial knowledge, Tahnee was able to learn more about what triggered her sensitivities and how to mitigate feeling overwhelmed. She and her grandmother became self-taught experts on the subject, and eventually Tahnee was able to find ways to enjoy her time with her grandparents to the fullest.

Tahnee's grandparents invited her to live with them if she decided to attend college. She talked about it with her parents and grandparents, and they felt this could be a good opportunity for her. As Tahnee thought about college, she considered a degree in illustration because drawing was a lifetime passion and she believed she would truly enjoy art classes. Tahnee began to research the program at a college near her grandparents' home. When planning her schedule, she made sure to give herself enough quiet downtime to balance her on-campus time. She recognized that she was less impacted by the outside world when she kept this balance.

After she moved to town and started classes, Tahnee found the adjustment to continuous city life to be stressful. Her grandmother convinced her to join a yoga class with her, and she felt it was a great stress reliever. She also began to try to meditate each day, and she got better and better at clearing her mind. Tahnee found she could use meditation to feel more relaxed when she was under deadlines or overtaxed by her environment. She knew her experience of growing up in the forest helped develop her sense of self and understand her baseline for feeling relaxed and comfortable.

Tahnee believed that if she had been raised in a typical suburban or urban environment, she would have been "a little crazy" and would never have experienced what it felt like to be at peace. Tahnee has learned that she needs rest time after doing activities that are filled with sensory stimuli. Knowing what she is like in the forest, compared with how she is in the "civilized" world, has allowed her to create that "forest feeling" when she needs it.

She also considered that "forest feeling" when she set up her room at her grandparents' home. She has a great deal of soft furniture, heavy blankets, layered carpets, and wall hangings that help to absorb sound. Tahnee uses lamps with low-watt, full-spectrum light bulbs and LED candles to replicate the softer glow of the lantern light of her childhood. When she is in this room, she sometimes plays audio recordings of birdsong or other sounds of nature, which help her to visualize her beloved forest.

After Tahnee graduated from college, her grandparents invited her to stay with them. This was mutually beneficial, as they could provide her with a rent-free work space and she could be there to help her grandparents as they aged. Tahnee wanted to build independence but knew this would be difficult for someone in their early 20s with no job experience. She was also worried about how the day-to-day requirement of working in an office would impact her energy and creativity. But retreating to the peace of her childhood home would not allow her the connectivity she needed to work. By staying in town with her grandparents, she was able to set up a studio with the level of technology she needed for freelance work.

Through her opportunities in the country and in town, Tahnee feels she has experienced the best of both worlds. She learned self-sufficiency at a young age through farm work with her parents; while living with her grandparents as a young adult has helped her adjust to the modern world. She appreciates that her grandparents are calm, patient people who have a slower pace of life, which offsets being in the city. She can go out with friends her own age, fully enjoying energetic activities, and then she can come home and decompress with her grandparents.

Tahnee and her grandparents have always communicated well and enjoy living together. They are kind to each other and try hard to be supportive. Together they have devised a way to share housekeeping duties that capitalize on each of their strengths. Tahnee does all of the quiet chores, such as sweeping, mopping, cleaning bathrooms, and washing windows. Her grandpa does the cooking and vacuuming, as he is not bothered by the sensory input of these activities. Her grandma manages the budget, takes care of any technological updates or problems, and buys the groceries. They have created a communal experience that works well for them.

All three work hard to be good housemates and are mindful of each other's needs and quirks. Tahnee's grandparents respect her level of sensitivity and give her quiet time to recharge. She has taken responsibility for finding ways that help adjust sound to tolerable levels. For example, she uses her earbuds to provide low background noise and sound regulation when she is in noisy environments.

They all go to visit Tahnee's family regularly and that gives Tahnee a chance to fully unwind. Her unique upbringing and supportive family have been the key to Tahnee's success so far. She is trying to figure out how she will integrate her two worlds to eventually live and work on her own. Tahnee would like to find a partner and raise her own family someday, so she is saving her money to build a tiny house on her parents' acreage. Tahnee wants to modernize her life on the farm somewhat, as she needs internet access and electricity to do her work. But she also wants to preserve the simplicity and connection to the land she loved as a child. She is grateful to have the freedom to create a lifestyle that gives her the flexibility to be independent but live within a community. Tahnee feels she has developed the tools to accommodate her needs and create a fulfilling life.

ADVICE

For many 2eA people, taking that step to adult life can be difficult, and may come at a later time. For those who have supportive parents, allowing yourself a longer time to launch into young adulthood can be helpful. 2eA people are often asynchronous in their development and may be intellectually far ahead of their peers, but socially or emotionally, their development may lag. They may need more time to get ready to go away to college, or to start a job, or even begin an entrepreneurial plan. Many don't feel they are really ready to begin adult life until their mid- to late 20s. Some don't have a supportive family and may be forced to begin living independently before they are ready. I have included some ideas below that may help with figuring out how to move into independent living, no matter how or when you do it.

~ Start with being aware of your own triggers. What makes you anxious or overwhelmed? Which types of environments sap your energy and leave you exhausted at the end of the day? Where do you feel most at ease and relaxed? What is it about that environment that is calming and restful? Understanding your own needs is the critical first step to building a safe haven. Many 2eA people have endured a lifetime of stressful environments, like school, work, or even at home. If at all possible, try to find simple ways to give yourself respite.

~ Once you discover the environmental elements that make a welcoming retreat from the world, begin to think about how to replicate them in your own home. For example, if glaring, fluorescent lights are exhausting, find ways to use natural light or soft lamp lighting instead of overhead fixtures. If you need total darkness to sleep, buy or make light blocking shades. If you are overwhelmed by too many items in your kitchen, keep your cupboards sparse. Even if you are sharing your home with others, you can still create spaces that give you respite and allow you to recharge. I know someone who created a sensory-free zone in his closet, so he can sit in this small, dim, quiet space when he feels dysregulated or exhausted.

~ If you live with other people, analyze what types of skills are required to do each chore. Divide the chores based on each person's strengths and abilities. If you are someone who easily loses track of time, being in charge of making dinner might not be a good job to tackle; but doing laundry could be better suited, as it may not be as time sensitive on a day-to-day basis.

~ Some of the most challenging parts of being a 2eA homekeeper come from dis/abilities and characteristics like ADHD, executive functioning, sensory-processing disorder, generalized anxiety disorder, depression, physical challenges, motivation, and boredom. Each of these will be addressed individually below with suggestions related to homekeeping. (If mental health issues are impacting your life overall, find a therapist who is an ally to help you work through them comprehensively.)

~ ADHD—for some people with ADHD, avoiding distraction and staying on task can be challenging, particularly if they live in a cluttered or overwhelming environment. For others, having all of the things they love clustered around them feels comforting. But if you find that you are unable to concentrate, or your room/home feels too distracting, you might follow the "less-is-more" lifestyle and create an organized, minimalist environment. Many 2eA people have difficulty parting with things, and this can lead to a cluttered home. Throwing out excess belongings can be the hardest part, so start with things you can sell or give away to friends or charities. Finding a good home for your things can help you to detach and move on with less anxiety. There are many systems for organizing your home, and you should find one that works best for you. The key is to start small, even if your first organization effort is one small drawer. Dividing your home into small areas to clean and organize can help you stay focused, and setting up a schedule can keep you on task. If you feel overwhelmed, only set up one task per day, and try to ignore anything that is not on your list.

~ Executive functioning—when you have difficulty organizing your thoughts and keeping track of necessary steps, homekeeping can be hard. Finding a way to list or chart your necessary chores can help. The less you have to store in your memory, the more functional you become. Creating a tangible, visual version of what you need to do, step by step, will help reduce your cognitive overload and allow you to focus on one step at a time. Organizational, visual planning apps like Tiimo[1] can be very effective in helping you to be more functional. (I am not being paid to promote anything in this book.)

~ Sensory processing—it is common for 2eA people to have sensory overexcitabilities, and the sounds, sights, and smells of cleaning can be difficult to endure. Think about how to reduce the sensory issues of each task, such as earplugs or noise-canceling headphones while you vacuum, or wearing a facemask to block smells when you take out the garbage, or putting on rubber gloves before you wash dirty dishes. Finding a way to put a protective barrier between yourself and the sensory trigger can make tasks feel more manageable.

~ Anxiety—fear, failure, and fear-of-failure can make tasks feel insurmountable. Your thoughts may begin to spin out of control as you face multiple tasks. You may feel that it is an all-or-nothing situation, but you don't have to do everything at once. When you feel anxious and find yourself procrastinating, pick one small item (especially something you enjoy) and do just that one thing to help

[1]   www.tiimoapp.com

counter your feeling of inertia. This can help to prevent you from starting a negative self-criticism cycle, which will ultimately make you feel like you are failing. Learn to embrace a "good enough" attitude to allow you to begin to break this anxiety loop. If certain tasks are more worrisome than others, start with the most doable tasks and work up to the difficult ones.

~ Depression—for many 2eA people, depression and anxiety are twin challenges. Depression can make it difficult to be functional in all areas of your life. Relying on kindness and support from others can be critical when you are finding that you just can't cope with daily stressors. Finding ways to value yourself and giving yourself a little grace can help reverse a downward spiral. Give yourself credit for even the smallest step you take each day.

~ Physical challenges—setting up your home to accommodate any mobility devices is something most people do when they move into a new home; but you can rethink how you use your home with mobility and functionality in mind. Imagine you have hired a person to professionally evaluate your home and make it more accommo-dating to your way of living. What would you tell them does and doesn't work? When you have identified the areas that are most dysfunctional, think about how you can tweak them to make them work better for you. You might find that moving furniture into a different configuration improves comfort, or moving items in your kitchen cupboards means less bending or reaching. Lowering or raising furniture heights, taking doors off cabinets, or grouping things you use together can increase functionality. Consciously considering how you move through your home, what activities you do throughout the day, and looking at the functionality of each room in your home can help to make it more accommodating and user-friendly.

~ Motivation—living in a world that feels out of sync with your needs can be very demoralizing. Many 2eA people seem to lack motivation, but it may actually be that you are overwhelmed with how much energy you need to expend to exist in the world. As a highly intellectual person, you may also lose motivation because you are chronically understimulated. If you don't have an opportunity to work, play, and interact in ways that feel authentic and stimulating, your motivation will be impacted.

~ Boredom—understimulation can also create feelings of boredom, but boredom does not have to be a negative experience. If you can view it as a precursor to creativity, it can make the experience less frustrating. From a mindfulness perspective, if you can allow yourself to sit with boredom for a period of time, it can take you into a creative space. According to Danckert and Eastwood (2020), boredom usually leads to daydreaming and that is the wellspring of creativity. Boredom can be a good way to reconnect with your authentic needs, as we need downtime to think and create.

Personal Care

❖❖❖

G UT PROBLEMS, restrictive eating, and food avoidance can be a barrier to adequate nutrition for many 2eA people. Sleep is hard to regulate. Allergies are common. And what if going to the doctor or dentist is such a sensory nightmare that you just can't bring yourself to do it? Or how can you be treated if you are hypersensitive to medication and no one believes your unusual side-effects? How do you care for a body that can seem alien and mutinous?

Mahlia

Mahlia has always had trouble with food. When she was a baby, she vomited after every feeding and her growth was impacted. Her Mom had to give her frequent smaller meals to try to help her keep food down. As a child, there were not many foods she liked to eat; and when she ate, she had trouble with her digestion. The texture and smell of many types of foods made her gag, making it impossible for her to eat them. She had particular difficulty with foods that were made of several components, like soups, stews, or salads. When her family ate those types of foods, she refused to come into the kitchen. All of her food had to be plain, simple, and kept separate on the plate.

During childhood, Mahlia saw a number of physicians, thera-pists, and specialists about her gut problems. She has always strug-gled with constipation, diarrhea, bloating, and nausea. Eventually, a gastrointestinal specialist diagnosed her with ulcerative colitis and prescribed medication. Swallowing pills was difficult for Mahlia, so her mother had to find ways to mix the medications with food. This further increased her anxiety about eating, as after taking her medication, Mahlia often had abdominal pain and discomfort.

Her Mom tried everything she could think of to increase the variety and amount of food Mahlia would eat, including attempts at hiding vegetable purees into baked treats or buying products that had increased protein, such as pasta made from chickpeas. But Mahlia regularly refused food and continued to grow at a slow rate. She was eventually diagnosed with avoidant/restrictive food intake disorder (ARFID) and was recommended to a pilot program through a university.

In this program, her parents learned new parenting skills to address issues with eating and food, while Mahlia's work focused on building tolerance and appetite through meal therapy and cog-nitive behavioral therapy (CBT). While she did improve her eating tolerance and anxiety management, Mahlia felt the program itself was a stressful experience. All of the eating exercises and pressures to follow the program's guidelines created a great deal of tension between Mahlia and her Mom.

Now that she is a young adult, eating is a topic that they have agreed not to discuss when Mahlia comes home to visit. She real-izes that this aspect of her childhood was particularly difficult for her Mom, as their culture places value on shared meals, hospitality to those who visit your home, and ensuring your children are al-ways well fed. Mahlia and her mother had many bitter fights about her refusal to eat most of the foods her Mom prepared. When she became an independent adult, it was one of the things Mahlia was most relieved to be freed from.

Living in her own home, she can control what and when she

eats, which has helped to relieve some of her anxiety about food. She does try to meet her basic nutritional needs and has done considerable research on her own about the typical gut problems experienced by autistic people, such as food sensitivities/allergies, intestinal pain/bloating, and constipation/diarrhea. Overall, Mahlia has not had a good experience with most medical professionals, as she finds they are quite uninformed when it comes to diet in general, but even more so when it comes to diet for people with autism. She has been pressured by more than one doctor to eat a greater variety of foods, despite growing evidence that most people who restrict their diet due to sensory issues still manage to meet their basic nutritional needs, and may naturally avoid food that could trigger sensitivity.

In her mid-20s, Mahlia chose to stop taking prescribed medications, and worked with a naturopath and nutritionist to try to build a healthy gut biome and deal with her digestive issues in a more holistic way. She feels that this has been somewhat successful, although she still has difficulty eating many of the probiotic and prebiotic foods that are recommended for this approach. She uses what she learned in her ARFID program to introduce some of these foods in very small quantities and eventually increase to larger portions, which helps her to build tolerance.

Mahlia has also had some success with using a meal replacement smoothie recipe she and her nutritionist developed. She finds she can tolerate this when other foods aren't palatable. "I actually wish I didn't have to eat. I don't find much pleasure in food, and psychologically, it has always felt a little traumatic." Not surprisingly, Mahlia is still considered underweight, and on some days, she doesn't have a great deal of energy. She is trying to increase the amount and variety of foods she eats, because she wants to take better care of her body overall, including having the stamina to exercise regularly.

Like so many 2eA people, Mahlia has extreme sensitivity to smell and taste. She also has some discomfort with touch. She feels she is like a dog when it comes to her sense of smell. Mahlia can smell things long before other people do, and certain strong smells, like chemicals or perfume, will give her an instant headache. While she also has sensitivity to touch and sound, her sensitivity to smell is what triggers her sensory overload most often. She is generally quite successful with social interactions but finds that the combined smells of people and shared food at gatherings makes her uncomfortable and nauseous.

Mahlia has developed some coping strategies for events that she is required to attend for work, such as putting a drop of scented oil on her upper lip and reapplying as necessary. While it doesn't completely block other smells, it does make them more tolerable. She tried many types of essential oil scents before she found one that worked for her, but once she did, it made socializing at parties less stressful. She also finds that she still uses techniques she learned through her childhood CBT work to manage intrusive or exaggerated thoughts when she is feeling socially anxious.

Mahlia is also working on her self-advocacy skills. She found that telling her supervisor she is 2eA has helped build awareness and support at work. But she is selective about who she shares her information with in general, as some people do not have a helpful response. Some people try to do too much accommodating, which makes Mahlia feel exposed, while others will exclude her if they feel something might be difficult for her. She understands that most people have good intentions, but they are often uninformed. Mahlia would prefer that people just proceed with their plans and let her decide what she needs to do to cope, or whether or not she feels comfortable attending. For the most part, she is pretty socially adept and feels that, in most cases, she can pass for "normal" and blend in with the crowd.

Mahlia also has to deal with another common misunderstanding about the reasons for her food aversions, that she is focused on being thin. The connection to body image and misogyny makes her angry. Mahlia is content with how she looks, but she has had to regularly contend with people who think it is about weight. She finds it both demeaning and annoying when people try to reassure her that she looks great or "is too thin to worry about her weight." This adds another layer of stress to her relationship with food and creates a deeper feeling of isolation from not being understood.

It is different with her close friends, as they know her well and she can be herself when she is with them. For example, she is a Dungeon Master (DM) for a group of friends who come to her house for weekly Dungeons and Dragons (D&D) games. Mahlia is a talented DM and spends a great deal of time creating worlds and scenarios that are fun and exciting for her players. She's glad that D&D is usually expected to be a food-free event, at least while the game is in play; but she also schedules the sessions for later in the evening to avoid the dinner hour. This allows her friends to eat before they come to play, and Mahlia doesn't feel pressure to provide post-game snacks.

She appreciates that they are supportive of her foodless events. She knows that food is a big part of many social gatherings but feels that she would be distracted throughout her game by worrying about post-game food. She doesn't want her own food issues to impact her ability to be an effective DM. "I put all my creative energy into my DMing and want to be on top of my game for my players. I am also a really active DM. I stand up, make big gestures, and run around to embody my NPCs,[1] so having food and drinks around could be dangerous."

Mahlia has always been hyper. As a child, she had trouble sitting still, so playing less active games, or just standing around talking with other children, didn't work well for her. In addition to her gut issues, hyperactivity is another physical trait that Mahlia shares with many autistic people. She also has sensory-processing disorder

---

1   Non-player character: any character in an MMORPG (massively multiplayer online role-playing game) that is controlled by the computer program, rather than by a human player.

(SPD), which affects her proprioception[2] and movement. When she was young, Mahlia frequently bumped into things, usually hard enough to leave a bruise. When she walked, her gait was sometimes uneven, and she often walked on her toes. Mahlia frequently got in trouble when playing with other children, as they complained that she was too rough in their physical games.

One of the many therapies Mahlia's Mom took her to when she was young was occupational therapy. She hoped it would help mitigate Mahlia's SPD and movement issues. The occupational therapist designed several therapeutic protocols to reduce Mahlia's sensitivity to touch and help her develop her motor skills. They were also given exercises they could do at home to support the occupational therapist's work, such as brushing therapy, and products like a weighted blanket, a sensory sock, ankle weights, and a compression vest. They found that the ankle weights helped Mahlia feel the most grounded and aware of where her body was within the environment during the day.

Mahlia believes her early occupational therapy interventions helped her sensory system to recalibrate somewhat and make daily life more tolerable. Many of the issues that were difficult for her as a child, such as teeth-brushing, clothing textures, and haircuts, are no longer as difficult in adulthood. "I still have to brace myself to endure a haircut, but most of the other sensory experiences that were such a nightmare in childhood are more like irritations now." She has been able to calm her sensory responses and feel more in control of her body, which makes most other aspects of her life a little easier.

She is able to adapt and adjust her surroundings to accommodate her needs most of the time. When she can't change the environment, she knows how to change her behaviors and expectations for herself. Mahlia is a great self-advocate and can tell others what she needs to be comfortable, while still respecting their hospitality or limitations. She has worked hard to build a social circle of true

2   The ability to sense the body's position and actions.

peers who understand and validate her needs. Mahlia feels that this self-knowledge has allowed her to be more engaged. She can even eat a traditional dinner with her Mom sometimes, which makes them both very happy.

Alden

When Alden is getting sick, he believes he can feel the difference between a bacterial and a viral infection. Bacterial infections create a feeling of lethargy that doesn't seem to be present with viral infections. He usually experiences that feeling before he has major symptoms, so it can be hard to convince doctors that he has an infection that might require antibiotics. He finds that they don't take his explanations seriously and often respond with basic explanations of symptoms or the differences between viruses and bacteria. Yet, Alden's self-diagnosis has nearly always been right.

He is sensitive in other ways too. Alden's body is highly impacted by what he eats, by the products he uses, and the medication he takes. His skin reacts to any perfumed products and his eyes water and his nose runs when he is around people who have used cologne or perfume. Foods with artificial ingredients taste metallic to Alden, and he feels irritable and out of sorts if he eats them. When he eats something very sugary, his upper lip begins to sweat, and he often feels nauseated. His body reacts differently to many over-the-counter medications too. Alden finds he experiences a lot of the listed side-effects, including some that are reported to happen only rarely.

Alden is also sensitive to levels of activity and environmental changes. He tries to walk every day for exercise, but knows, if he does too much, he will have extreme fatigue the next day. If he spends too much time in bright light, he will suffer from headaches, so he rarely goes outside without a hat and sunglasses. When the seasons change, Alden can feel his body respond. He has seasonal affective disorder and fights depression throughout the winter months.

Alden feels that most professionals disregard his complaints and how he describes symptoms as exaggerated or overreactive. "Lots of people think I am a hypochondriac, which makes it even more difficult to explain what is happening in my body." He is envious of people whose bodies seem to be unaffected and resilient. Alden has tried a wide variety of diets and lifestyle recommendations in an effort to improve his overall health and well-being. Over the years, he has determined what seems to work best for his body, but nothing has ever helped him to feel he has robust health.

Many aspects of the world make it feel like a hostile place for Alden. His childhood experiences taught him that he must remain vigilant to avoid a wide spectrum of potentially harmful situations. Alden has many characteristics that made his earlier life difficult. He suffered from allergies to pollen and always had a runny nose and itchy eyes. He also had a strong gag reflex, and the sight or smell of certain foods that others were eating could trigger vomiting. Alden was small for his age and talked in a high, sing-song voice. He describes his younger self as a "tiny, odd child" who looked, sounded, and acted differently. Alden was an easy target for bullies.

He tried to isolate himself as much as possible when he was at school. "I knew all the best hiding spots, so I would tuck myself away from others to feel safe during recess. I was always the last one back into the classroom, and I got scolded a lot; but that was better than getting bullied." The classroom was a safer place for Alden, as he was a gifted student who could easily complete his schoolwork. It also helped that he was polite to adults and very compliant in the classroom. He usually found allies in his teachers, who were often champions for the underdog.

Alden plodded through his elementary and middle-school years and finally found that things got a little better in high school. He was able to attend a specialized high school for gifted students and enjoyed the accelerated learning environment. He felt less atypical in this setting and was relieved that he blended in a bit more. Alden still continued to feel more comfortable keeping his distance, and other students generally left him alone.

Alden had always loved designing and building constructions. He also enjoyed sketching futuristic homes and eventually learned how to draw computer-aided design (CAD) floorplans. In high school he gravitated toward architecture and was able to take advanced design classes. Alden was fascinated with Jacque Fresco's Venus Project[3] and wanted to create a career in "sociocyberengineering" to design more sustainable communities.

He found a university that offered a sustainable community development degree program. Alden's degree allowed him to focus on building environments that help to regenerate the health of the planet. He was particularly interested in finding ways to integrate communities into the land through supporting ecosystem rehabilitation, such as community gardens or farmers markets in urban food deserts. Through his university courses, Alden was able to study projects around the world that focused on biodiversity, agroforestry, carbon sequestration, and permaculture.

Part of his early fascination with sociocyberengineering was exploring how humans impact the health of the planet, which, in turn, impacts human health. Alden envisioned a community that could optimize the health and well-being of everyone and everything. He wanted a place in the world where people like him could lead healthy, productive lives. Alden believed that reducing stress on as many fronts as possible would help his body to be less reactive to the remaining stressors. His community was designed to reduce pollution, work stress, and consumption, while increasing community interaction, a local resource-based economy, and sustainable housing.

After graduation, Alden's dream began to take shape when he joined a community of like-minded people who were building a

3   www.thevenusproject.com

thoughtfully planned eco-village on an acreage donated for their experimental work. The community considered their village a living lab, designed to research solutions for collapsing ecosystems, diminishing resources, and social equality challenges. Their mission was to view life as integrated and holistic, which aligned with Alden's dream of living in a place that is both progressive and healing.

Through conversations with his fellow villagers, Alden could see that there was something to be learned from ancient wisdom too. He was impressed with the success of their efforts to combine old ways with new knowledge throughout their project. For example, they have built chinampas (floating gardens designed by the Aztecs) to research the sustainability of this type of garden. They are trying various building materials, like cob (a mixture of straw and mud), to find the most energy efficient options. Alden also enjoys the spiritual aspects of their lifestyle. He has met people who practiced Ayurvedic medicine, herbal remedies, periodic fasting, and mind/body connection through meditation. The more he learned, the more Alden became aware of his body and how to recognize subtle signals of what his body needed and to respond accordingly.

Over the next few years, Alden began to eat a simple, close-to-nature diet of locally grown food. He tried to balance his physical activity with regular rest periods and found his stamina improved. His allergies improved and working outside became a source of pleasure. Alden feels that he will always have to be mindful of his physical limitations, but he believes that he is stronger and healthier living this new life. He has changed old patterns of anxiety that were related to feeling out of control. The more he has learned about exercising his body and calming his mind, the less sick and anxious he has become.

Alden is also more socially involved with his fellow villagers now, as they all contribute through various shared work programs. Alden enjoys discussions and planning sessions, as many of his community are intelligent, creative people who are inclusive and open-minded. He is inspired by their combined research work and hopes to be able to teach others how to replicate their successes. Despite the closeness of the community, Alden also finds he has enough time and space for rest and solitude. This gives him a sense of balance and increases his ability to contribute overall. "When you are able to focus on what really matters to you, the rest kind of falls into place. I live in a village where we are all trying to make things better for everyone, and that positivity is healing."

ADVICE

~ Many 2eA people can compensate for the difficult parts of being 2eA, often so well that others don't understand how hard they are working to mask their struggles. You may be seen as someone who is coping well and not get the support you actually need. Feeling like you are not believed or having your problems dismissed can be debilitating. It can help to find/create a community where you don't have to mask your behaviors or identity.

~ Another barrier to getting good medical/therapeutic care is the lack of professionals who have deep knowledge about 2eA issues. They often don't understand the typical social, emotional, and in-tellectual behaviors and needs of 2eA people and may misdiagnose and mistreat them.

~ Anything you can do to increase your physical comfort will help with sensory overload. If you find clothing that feels right, buy it in multiple. Depending on your work environment, you may be able to wear a clean version of the same clothing every day. It might even become your trademark look, like Steve Jobs' black t-shirts and old jeans.

~ Diet can be problematic for 2eA people, as food allergies and in-tolerances are common. You may have to try elimination diets, or introduce new foods one at a time, to see what your digestive system will tolerate.

~ Try to find ways to include healthy foods, particularly fruits and vegetables, in ways that are palatable. You can find recipes on how to include pureed fruits and vegetables in baked goods and entrees. The more varieties of produce you eat, the broader spectrum of nutrients your body has to function well. This also helps to build a healthy gut biome.

~ Look for blogs or YouTube channels to learn how to source foods and cook meals that fit your dietary needs (such as gluten-free, dairy-free, vegan, or reduced sugar).

~ Look for alternative hygiene and grooming products that are not overwhelming to your senses (such as using child's fruit-flavored toothpaste instead of typical adult peppermint).

~ Create a sensory-calming environment that is simple and mini-malistic. Some common problems are: fluorescent lights (humming sound, flickering light), busy wallpaper/carpet patterns or too bright paint colors, too much background noise, lights that are too bright or wavelength is wrong, smells and scents from products or cook-ing, fabric on furnishings that is rough or scratchy, and over-fur-nished or visually busy décor.

~ 2eA people may be hypersensitive to physical sensations, so stub-bing your toe or being clapped on the back can cause more extreme startle or pain response. Help those around you understand your responses and be respectful of your needs. Learn ways to cope with momentary pain, such as squeezing pressure points, deep breathing, or movement techniques.

~ Trust your sensations. If you feel something is not right in your body, be persistent in finding a sensitive medical practitioner who will partner with you in improving and maintaining your health.

~ Learn as much as you can about your body: What do you feel like when you are relaxed and calm? What is your baseline for health and fitness? What are your body's signals that you are getting sick or overstressed?

~ Try different approaches to preventative self-care to find what works best for you. Be open to new ideas and processes that might increase your comfort, health, and well-being.

~ If you suffer from chronic pain, investigate alternative, holistic approaches to pain management. Most traditional medical treatments do not work well for chronic pain, as they do not target both the brain and the body. Dr. Rachel Zoffness is a leading pain psychologist who has provided many resources for effective pain management, see www.zoffness.com.

~ Western medicine has traditionally viewed mental and physical health as two distinct areas of care. There is an increasing movement to integrate care, as the mind and body are not separate. Many 2eA people are highly impacted by physical and emotional stressors and need to address the root causes of those stressors to promote optimal wellness. Work to identify problems and address them through integrative care.

Having Fun

O NLINE COMMUNICATION, interest groups, and gaming is a boon for many 2eA people, as it allows them to connect to others in a way that feels safe. But finding people who share your interests, accept your quirks, and enjoy your company in the real world can be challenging. Face-to-face emotions can be too intense and relationships overwhelming, but that doesn't take away the longing for inclusion or the desire to find friends.

Jonathan

Jonathan used to be an aggressive person. His elementary school years were fraught with being sent to the principal's office or going home for physical or verbal aggression toward his teachers and peers. Middle school was the hardest time for him, as school administration was less tolerant of his behaviors and punishment was more severe. He had several suspensions and was nearly expelled in eighth grade; but no one ever attributed his behaviors to a dis/ability. He was seen as a behavioral challenge, a difficult kid. There was no awareness that he might need extra support, or even that he was struggling every day. He was one of the unlucky kids whose behavior made the adults around him want to increase discipline or punishment, rather than foster empathy.

Like many 2eA people, Jonathan is very sensitive to environmental stressors and experiences high levels of anxiety when he is overwhelmed. In addition, he was teased in early elementary and reacted physically to the taunting. Jonathan was a big kid, taller and stronger than many of his peers, so fighting back often meant that he was seen as the aggressor. He has always had difficulty finding the right words to express what he is feeling, and when he is under duress, he usually cannot speak at all.

All of these factors combined to make his educational years difficult, both academically and socially. Jonathan's parents knew he wanted friends and tried to find ways to foster friendships and join activities that might be inclusive. But they also knew that his emotional dysregulation and reactivity caused many of their efforts to be in vain. While Jonathan did not have a high social drive or want a large circle of friends, he always wanted at least one friend, and was lonely for most of his childhood.

In high school, Jonathan got into a fight with another student and a teacher was slightly injured when he tried to break it up. The school required Jonathan to see a therapist as part of the conditions he needed to meet to remain at school. Fortunately, the therapist was familiar with the needs of both gifted and autistic people, so was able to recognize the underlying anxiety and sensory problems that led to Jonathan's behavioral issues. She knew that when he is worried about an assignment or stressed by the noisy classroom, he is much more likely to be reactive to a peer's comment or teacher's demand. Jonathan met with his therapist on a weekly basis throughout most of his high-school years. He feels that this is what allowed him to finally understand his experiences and develop healthier coping skills. Ultimately, this led to a change in behavior that allowed him to be more functional.

What Jonathan feels he has missed is the relational learning that happens through friendships. He never had any close friends during his school years and that left him with some deficits in his pro-social skills.[1] He had to learn these skills as a young adult, often through trial and error, and it was difficult for him. For example, in his first year at college, Jonathan shared an apartment on campus with three other people. He struggled with understanding basic roommate etiquette, such as wiping your toothpaste splatters off the bathroom mirror, giving privacy to a roommate who was entertaining someone, or being aware of your night-time noise levels. He received a great deal of negative feedback from his room-mates and often felt bewildered and overwhelmed by the unwritten social rules.

His second year at college was better, as the university opened an autism support center and Jonathan was able to utilize their classes and personnel to help him learn to navigate a wider variety of social situations. He felt that he grew his skills considerably, but still had difficulty finding friends. When he began his third year at college he began to take more classes related to his major, political science. Jonathan found himself surrounded by more like-minded people, and, in many cases, others who were as passionate about politics and social justice as he was. The coursework also began to involve more extracurricular projects and group activities, which naturally expanded Jonathan's social interactions. He found ways to channel his energy into meaningful work with intellectual equals.

College gave Jonathan a place to try new things, make mistakes, and figure himself out. For example, Jonathan took a debate class and found that researching and debating topics was both intellec-tually exciting and enlightening. He credits that class for helping him to better understand multiple perspectives. When he had to debate opposite sides of a topic for his course, something clicked for Jonathan. "I finally got that being in a relationship required me to let go of some of my rigidity and acknowledge another person's

---

1   Pro-social skills: social skills that are related to finding and maintaining relationships, particularly in a deeply connected way. For example, positive skills and attributes that promote healthy attachment, such as the ability to take another's perspective.

point of view. My parents had been trying to teach me this for years, but I was finally able to see it in my own life."

Additionally, Jonathan had always believed that he was a shy person until he took the debate class. He found that he liked defending his argument and enjoyed being the center of attention during those moments. In an indirect way, this gave him confidence to be more outspoken about his own thoughts and ideas when he was in a social group. Eventually, he started a board game night at his dorm that became a well-attended, enjoyable activity. Jonathan loved weird old board games, so he challenged others to bring a game that was retro, unknown, funny, or just plain strange. He had quite a few games he had collected over the years, so was able to start with those; but then his fellow gamers really stepped up to the challenge. It became something he looked forward to at the end of each week.

Jonathan developed in other non-academic ways too. One of his professors offered extra credit for those who volunteered at the campus food bank garden. He found he really enjoyed the camaraderie and physical work at the garden. He even learned some basic cooking skills from fellow gardeners, as they often prepared a meal together at the end of their workday using the surplus harvest. Jonathan eventually decided to become vegan, as it resonated with his love for animals and desire to live in a sustainable way. He feels his current healthy lifestyle is directly linked to that year he worked at the garden. "There was something about eating food I helped to grow that allowed me to expand my palate. I began to eat better than I ever had in the past."

His stronger social skills also gave Jonathan confidence to advocate for himself. He became more adept at telling his peers about his needs and explaining how to mitigate triggers. For example, they now knew that he would be less talkative and involved if there were a large number of people or a noisy event. They began to understand that small groups or quieter venues allowed Jonathan to engage fully and be in his most responsive state. For the most part, Jonathan found people were understanding and supportive, particularly as he became better at understanding and accommodating their needs too.

He was pretty hard on himself in his late teens and early 20s. He felt like he would never be good at figuring out social demands. Jonathan worried a lot about never being able to find a girlfriend, or not having friends to hang out with. Looking back, he could see that many of these skills just take time and practice to develop. "You have to be okay with putting yourself out there knowing that some people are going to reject you no matter what. Once I got over feeling like there was something wrong with me, I saw that everybody has some insecurity about friendship and romance."

Jonathan was able to develop a more positive self-image, which helped him to be less anxious and comfortable with communicating his needs. The more competent he felt in his social skills, the better he became at deepening relationships and developing pro-social skills; which, in turn, helped him successfully build meaningful connections to others. For example, Jonathan began to remember to check in with a friend who was sick or ask how another's new job was going. He got better at apologizing when he was wrong, remembering to thank people, or supporting someone else's ideas.

He could see that people are attracted to those who are confident, energetic, positive, and kind. Jonathan believed that he was naturally energetic and kind, and willing to work on developing his confidence and positivity. This self-awareness helped him find ways to put himself out there and attract friends among his cohorts of fellow students. He became the guy who suggested going to check out a new food truck for lunch break or offer to help coordinate a study group.

Like all people, finding those who shared his interests gave Jonathan a community of true peers and allowed him to develop deeper friendships. For many 2eA people, this feeling of inclusion is a new experience. For Jonathan, it was a significant confidence booster and contributed to his decision to pursue advanced degrees. His greater self-confidence allowed him to pursue and complete his doctorate in political science in his early 30s. By this time, Jonathan had several close friends and had been in one romantic relationship. He was confident in his socializing and happy to have friends, even if it was difficult or painful at times. He felt like he was participating in life, finally catching up on all those experiences he had missed out on when he was young.

Jonathan has been able to adjust his expectations over the years, as he learned to accept his asynchronous development. His intellectual abilities always preceded his social and emotional growth. He believes that he is beginning to be more aligned in all three areas now, even though he is still impacted by aspects of his 2eA profile. He has a fairly accurate understanding of what he needs to accentuate his abilities and support his dis/abilities. He knows that he needs a quiet time to prepare for, or recover from, the days he must be functional in meetings or conferences.

Jonathan understands that some things will always require extra effort and adaptation, as most of his environments are not built with 2eA needs in mind. But he feels confident that he can just quietly deal with some challenges, and fully advocate for himself with others. He has also created space at work and at home that provide varying levels of respite and safety. Jonathan believes that the secret to succeeding as a 2eA person is finding out what causes problems for you, and then proactively building systems and finding allies who can help you overcome those hurdles.

Mimi

Mimi has been highly creative and sensitive from a very young age. As a toddler, she had regular, energetic talks with her imaginary friend. By preschool she was known for her long and involved stories about fantastical creatures and the worlds they inhabited. When she was four, she pestered her parents to teach her to write so she could record the stories that went with her drawings. It became clear that Mimi was a gifted child, as not only did she learn to write, but she also rapidly learned to read. Reading enhanced her storytelling, as she could now read many stories on her own. She could tell rich, deeply imaginative stories that were impressive in length, plot, and detail. Some of her stories had themes from books she read, but most of them were her own creations. Her parents thought her precocious creativity was wonderful and encouraged her to continue drawing and writing her stories.

Mimi also liked to make up games and direct her parents in how they should play. Sometimes her games and stories overlapped as she wrote episodes that included her parents to play roles in her imaginary games. They were amused at her wild imagination and indulged her by listening to her stories and playing the games she invented. While Mimi could be intense, she was also a sweet and thoughtful child, who noticed when people were sad or hurt and tried to help them feel better. Her stories often had themes of rescuing helpless animals or taking action to make things better. Her parents were proud of their smart, inventive, and sensitive girl.

As she approached school age, her parents looked forward to enrolling her in their neighborhood school. They knew she would excel academically, since she already knew how to read and write well above grade level. They also expected that she would find friends, as she was outgoing and full of fun ideas. Mimi was excited to start school, she looked forward to having friends to play with and a teacher to help her learn.

However, once she started school, Mimi was surprised to find that her classmates didn't share her ideas of what she thought was fun. They didn't want to listen to her in-depth stories or abide by the specific rules to her imaginary games. When she got upset that her peers didn't do as she asked, the teachers told her that her friends didn't like to always follow her lead. They reminded her that she needed to learn to take turns and let others have a chance to be the leader in the games.

But when Mimi followed the other children's lead, she found their stories and games to be predictable and boring. She was often frustrated by the repetition of their games and lost interest in playing the same types of stories over and over again. Mimi continued to try to recruit people to play her way, but the more she insisted, the less interested they became. When she argued and cried to get her way, they began to make fun of her, belittling her stories and calling her names. Initially, Mimi staunchly defended her imaginary worlds and their inhabitants, but eventually the continual rejection began to take its toll.

Her parents could see that she was struggling socially and tried to intervene to help her have better interactions. They set up playdates and talked with her about her feelings and actions. They worked to build her social skills and help her understand what she needed to do to be a good friend. But Mimi was adamant about others doing things her way and got extremely upset when anyone tried to change the rules. She was not able to be flexible and accommodating, and often had melt downs when trying to control others.

Her rigidity also began to spread to her interactions in the classroom and at home. Mimi became a perfectionist about her schoolwork and spent an inordinate amount of time completing her work. She was obsessed with how things were arranged in her room and got very upset if her parents moved anything around. Mimi began to refuse to play with friends and spent a great deal of her free time playing Minecraft on her iPad. Her parents felt that they were missing some critical clue about how to help her succeed.

At her annual checkup at the end of her kindergarten school year, her parents told the pediatrician about her behaviors. The doctor suggested that Mimi might be on the autism spectrum and/or highly gifted. She referred them for assessment and the results showed that Mimi was both autistic and gifted, which explained her overexcitabilities, intensities, and perfectionism. Mimi's parents felt it was important to tell her that her brain was wired a little differently and hoped it would help her to understand her abilities and difficulties. It did not have the intended effect, as Mimi began to worry about being different and told her parents she wanted a "normal brain."

When Mimi started first grade, she no longer told stories or tried to direct games at school. She abandoned her imaginary worlds and began to try harder to assimilate into her peer group. She toned down her intensity and kept her ideas to herself. She became quieter and more withdrawn, often spending recess watching the other children play. Mimi took notice of how they behaved and tried to figure out how to be more like them. She hung around on the fringes of the groups of children, trying to fit in.

Mimi began to conform in class too. Her writing changed to be more like the other children's stories, filled with kittens and trips to the beach instead of strange worlds occupied by wild creatures. Mimi's parents noticed that she lost interest in writing and illustrating her stories at home too. They were sad to see that she no longer asked them to play in her imaginary games. She told them her stories were stupid baby stories and she didn't like them anymore.

As first grade progressed, Mimi suppressed her urge to add details or contribute ideas to the other children's games. She became a follower who did what others wanted her to do when they played. In the classroom, Mimi completed her schoolwork exactly as instructed and focused on producing perfect work. She began to blend in. Her teachers were pleased. They felt her social skills were improving and she was becoming a well-rounded student.

However, at home, Mimi had more frequent outbursts and tantrums. Her parents adjusted their approach to set more consistent expectations, rewards, and limits, hoping this would help Mimi to regulate her behaviors. They signed up for parenting classes for parents of autistic children, and enrolled Mimi in social groups and behavioral therapy. Eventually, their efforts did help, as Mimi's tantrums became less frequent, but the pattern of blending in at school, and acting out at home, continued throughout her childhood and early teen years.

By high school, Mimi had succeeded in reining in her emotions, but this brought another layer of complexity. The more she suppressed her emotions, the more she began to suffer from anxiety. She was inordinately worried about saying or doing something that might be wrong or could impact others. She also felt bombarded by others' emotions, which was overwhelming and exhausting. She could just be walking to class and experience flashes of sorrow, anger, excitement, or joy, a kaleidoscope of emotions that didn't seem to have anything to do with her own reality. To process her feelings, Mimi began to keep journals filled with art and occasional commentary on her experiences.

Her intuition was greater with people she had relationships with, and she often had flashes of insight about friends' and family members' problems but didn't feel comfortable sharing her suggestions. Mimi kept all of these experiences to herself, but often felt like a chameleon, seeming to absorb and reflect others' emotions. At times, she began to doubt whether her feelings were actually her own. Mimi started to feel like an imposter in her own life, and sometimes she worried she might have a mental illness.

After she graduated from high school, with young adulthood looming, Mimi experienced increasing anxiety and difficulty with social demands. She started to see a therapist, but her therapist had set ideas about her needs as a gifted person who also has autism. Mimi struggled to explain herself to her therapist but often felt she was misunderstood. She was rarely comfortable enough to reveal the extent of her experiences with emotional downloading. Mimi was afraid that her therapist would think she was making it up. For the most part, Mimi tried to deal with her reality on her own, only talking about certain parts of it to her therapist when she had experienced a particularly exhausting or anxious encounter.

Then one day Mimi found a podcast about empaths and was astonished to hear them discuss their experiences. It seemed like they were describing her own life. "I felt the shock of recognition, but I was stunned that they spoke about it as if it were an acceptable way to be." The podcast recommended reading *The Empath's Survival Guide* by Dr. Judith Orloff, and Mimi immediately went out and bought the book. As she read, Mimi found that there were many explanations for how empaths experience the world. It was the first time she understood that her giftedness might be related to her empathy. Mimi was also surprised to learn that having a high sensitivity to others' emotions was also a common empathic trait.

The more Mimi learned about herself, the more excited she became to meet others like her. She joined an online empath group and attended every conference or seminar she could find on empathic phenomena. As she began to develop relationships with fellow empaths, Mimi felt pride in her unique abilities for the first time in her life. She became better at not absorbing the emotions of others and learned more about her overexcitabilities, insights, and intuition. Mimi began to recognize the impact of other people's energies and how to protect herself from being overwhelmed by those around her. She became aware of which situations and people sapped her energy and how to recharge through practices like visualization and deep breathing.

Mimi also began to see the possibilities for using her gifts to earn a living, while also helping others. She saw other empaths who did everything from psychic readings to psychotherapy. She met people who did body work such as Reiki, healing massage, or Jin Shin Jyutsu. Mimi learned that many empaths used their creative sensitivity and insight to build careers in music, writing, and art. Others focused on healing through nursing, teaching, or hospice work.

Exploring the pathways of others allowed Mimi to analyze her own strengths and limitations. She considered several careers that seemed interesting and complementary to her abilities. Mimi considered working as an author, a yoga instructor, or a doula, but none of those seemed quite right. Eventually Mimi decided to become an art therapist, a job that would allow her to use both her artistic skills and her ability to read and respond to emotion. When she finished her undergraduate degree, Mimi found an art therapy master's degree program at a nearby university and enrolled.

As she progressed through her education, Mimi was pleased to find that she crossed paths with fellow empaths in her program. She also found friends who were not empaths, but kindred spirits in other ways, such as having a shared love of art. Mimi began to build strong friendships and enjoy activities with her peers. She had friends who shared her love of nature and joined her for landscape-painting excursions. Others met for a monthly dinner out or gallery walk. The most comforting commonality with all her friends was their acceptance of her abilities and history. Mimi could openly discuss her experiences and feel accepted and understood. She appreciated that her friends got her frequent need for quiet decompression after a day of class or clinical work. When she was struggling, they often suggested just the right thing to help her feel grounded, such as a visit to a botanical garden or joining them for a cup of tea.

She also appreciated that she could reciprocate and repay their kindness through utilizing her talents. Mimi could offer insight into their worries or notice changes to their countenance. She was a good listener, and her friends could feel her love and concern for them as they shared their problems. Mimi tried to be a conduit for greater good, supporting her friends as they made mistakes and worked to overcome hardships. She was a compassionate friend, and a great shoulder to cry on. She also knew when to step back and respect her own boundaries for self-care. Her good energy was appreciated by all of her friends, and she was able to be her best self because they understood her need for time and space to recharge.

Through recognizing and embracing her exceptional abilities, Mimi has built a successful art-therapy practice, found a close circle of friends, and continues to work toward a balanced life. She has found a way to capitalize on her differences that is both lucrative and fulfilling. Most days, Mimi feels empowered to be herself. She now tries to surround herself with empaths and allies, which she feels both increases her ability to function and provides a protective layer from intensity. "I love that so many of my friends have experienced the same things I have. We look out for each other during the rough times, and we can be blissfully in-tune on the good days."

Since she no longer expends so much energy trying to fight who she is, Mimi is excited about being 2eA and has become an outspoken enthusiast about her neurodiversity and the potential it represents for helping others. "Imagine if we taught children about the many types of gifts they might have. I would have had a much less stressful childhood if I had known that there were other people just like me. That's why I want everyone to embrace their weirdness and be proud, unapologetic 2eA empaths. I think we should let our freak flags fly!"

ADVICE

~ Socializing is often an area of struggle for many 2eA people. You may have past negative experiences with ostracization or bullying, or you might lack confidence because you haven't had much practice. You can replace those past experiences with more positive interactions through carefully planned interactions and activities as an adult.

~ Many 2eA people find socializing to be a stressful or unpleasant activity because they are not sure what is expected or how to fit in at many gatherings. It can be helpful to socialize around a specific goal-oriented activity. This can reduce social anxiety through the structure of the activity and the shared interest of the people attending. You may have specific friend groups that you see for specific activities, which can expand your relationships and provide satisfactory interactions.

~ Know your triggers and do what you need to make yourself comfortable in social situations. For example, if you know an event will be noisy, wear earplugs; if eye contact is overwhelming, wear tinted glasses; if talking on the phone is difficult, communicate through text. The more comfortable you are, the more engaged your mind will be, and that will usually make the event more fun.

~ Social anxiety and fear of the unknown can make you miss out on things you would like to do, try, or learn. Planning ahead, thinking through expectations, and taking small steps toward gaining confidence can help you to break through the fear barrier. For example, if you have always wanted to go to a Maker Fair but the crowds feel too overwhelming, find a smaller, similar venue like a mini-Maker event or a Maker class to start. Try attending for just 15 minutes before retreating to a safer, quieter place. Go with a trusted ally who can help if you start to feel panic. Gear up with earplugs, a compression vest, or ankle weights, use whatever tools you know will help reduce the sensory input or physical overwhelming aspect of the event.

~ Find ways to socialize that allow you to be in your safe space, such as playing online games, joining groups around shared interests, or activities that give you a protective persona, like a game avatar or costume at a con.[2]

~ Social politics and group dynamics can make trying to fit in feel insurmountable. You may be more successful in socializing in small groups of one or two other people where the conversation can be more meaningful and the inter-group connections and interactions less complicated. You may even find others who enjoy companionable, side-by-side activities that do not require constant conversation and interaction.

---

2   A convention centered around special interests, such as comic books or anime. Some of the most well known are Comiccon, Gamescon, Dragon Con, Comiket, PAXPrime, MegaCon, and Anime Expo.

~ Neurotypical life may seem irrational and many customs and be-haviors appear pointless to 2eA people. It can be helpful to accept that not everything can be explained logically and work on letting go of control about what others do.

~ Try to be open to new experiences. You may feel anxiety about novel experiences, lack of competency, or perceived discomfort; but trying something new can allow you to find previously un-tapped strengths and help increase tolerance and resilience.

~ Don't be too hard on yourself. Many 2eA people's anxiety and perfectionism rolls into their socializing and they hold themselves to unrealistic standards. Everyone has moments of awkward inter-actions, failed attempts, and rejection.

~ Not all 2eA people want to socialize on a regular basis. Many enjoy solitary activities and the quiet, relaxed aspect of being on your own. Don't let others pressure you to socialize if you prefer a more introverted life. You have the right to relax and have fun however you see fit.

Dating and Sex

H OW DO YOU LEARN to connect, express yourself, or offer commitment if you haven't had any practice with developing and maintaining relationships? What if you can't make small talk or understand the nuances of flirting? For 2eA people, sex can be over-stimulating, uninteresting, or too conformist. Others' emotional needs can feel unmanageable when you can't even figure out how to process your own. Finding a soulmate is a multilayered maze that is often fraught with failure for many 2eA people.

Xena

Xena is a complex, genderqueer[1] person who refuses to be defined by traditional norms and has chosen to use the pronouns "ze/hir" when referring to self. Ze is a talented artist who loves to learn about the cultural history and behaviors of people across the world. Xena chooses to dress in many forms, at times a Victorian suffragette, at others an Edwardian dandy man, or a 1950s housewife. Ze loves costuming and has an extensive wardrobe of carefully constructed, historically accurate clothing. Hir interest started young,

---

1   Genderqueer: someone who rejects conventional gender roles and distinctions. They do not identify as exclusively male or female; rather, they may be either, both, neither, or a combination at any given time.

as ze was into cosplay during hir teens, and this passion carried Xena into a career in costume design. Ze is a walking advertisement of hir skills, as every outfit ze wears is beautifully researched and constructed. Xena feels that hir true self has many faces and should be honored through what ze wears.

Ze is equally complex in hir thoughts and beliefs. Xena is a highly creative person who has always rejected being compartmentalized by others. From an early age, ze refused to be gendered. Hir parents were sometimes exasperated but tried to be supportive. Extended family members were less open and accepting. Ze was often scolded by hir grandparents who insisted ze was a girl and should act like one. Xena was also teased and bullied at times by peers, who saw hir as an easy target because of hir outspoken activism.

While this was a difficult experience when ze was young, ze now feels this ability has shaped hir outlook on the world. Xena understands that most people don't reject norms as ze does, as they usually conform to societal pressures in many areas of their lives. Ze knows that hir early activism is unusual and it has taken hir many years to learn how to ground hirself and release the expectations of others. When Xena was a child, ze would often feel rage at the narrow-mindedness of people, without knowing how to explain its impact.

Hir parents were often concerned about hir emotional state and ze saw several therapists throughout hir childhood. Initially, the therapeutic work was centered more around hir autism than hir gender and body activism. For Xena, this was just another form of compartmentalizing humans, and ze became disenchanted with therapy in general. In hir late teens, ze eventually found a therapist who specialized in helping young genderqueer people with identity development through a focus on activism. This gave Xena a forum for refining how ze wanted to be in the world.

Fortunately for Xena, hir parents were also supportive of hir gender explorations. Even when ze was younger, they allowed hir to dress as a boy sometimes, as a girl at other times, or in neutral costumes, always advocating for hir individuality and right to self-expression at school. As Xena's tastes became more eclectic, hir parents didn't restrict hir creativity or the activism ze conveyed through hir wardrobe.

By middle school Xena was a regular thrift store shopper and had begun to hone hir sewing skills through reconstructing hir purchases into unique outfits. Hir parents helped hir pursue this passion through providing clothing design and construction lessons. By high school, Xena's clothing had begun to take on hir signature historical style. Ze began to post hir creations on social media and credits the eventual popularity of hir sites for hir present-day occupation.

Hir social media following also gave hir a platform to advocate for recognition and equality for hir communities, 2eA and LGBTQ. Xena strongly identifies with the movement toward acceptance and celebration of all humans, however they choose to express themselves. Hir sexuality is also expressed in a fluid and non-conforming way. Xena does not limit hirself to any one practice or label but has followed hir desire without concern for classification. Xena has loved people who were pan, demiboy/girl, null gender, gay, straight, bi, and trans. Ze doesn't understand why others limit themselves, as ze finds all types of people attractive and interesting.

Xena knows that many in hir 2eA community have had difficulty with dating, sex, and relationships. Some are gullible and easily manipulated by others, experiencing harm because they are vulnerable. When Xena was in hir 20s, ze had a relationship with hir supervisor at work. Ze considered this person as a mentor and someone who could help hir learn hir trade. Xena is beautiful. Hir androgynous physical traits are a perfect blank canvas for hir costuming.

Ze draws a lot of attention wherever ze goes, but not all of it has been good for hir. Looking back, ze knows that hir supervisor took advantage of hir and preyed upon hir lack of experience. "I worshipped him! He was everything I wanted to be, funny, successful, talented, and admired. But he was not a good person. He took advantage of my innocence, both sexually and professionally.

He regularly cheated on me and often took credit for my ideas at work. He broke my heart. I learned a great deal about what to avoid the next time!"

Xena feels that ze has relatively good social skills. There are times when ze finds hirself feeling anxious and out of hir depth, particularly in larger social gatherings. When there are many conversations and interactions happening around hir, Xena tends to feel overwhelmed and often needs to take quiet breaks during the event. Ze has gotten better at focusing on one person or a small group of people within the larger milieu, but still finds parties exhausting. "There is a huge amount of sorting and processing of what is being said, what is meant by what is said, and how you are supposed to interpret what is said. If you layer trying to read body language and facial expressions on top of that, it is just complete overload."

Xena knows that ze has always struggled to understand the nuances of what is being said, such as deciphering meaning from more nuanced languaging, like voice tone or facial micro-expression. Ze is also often surprised by the difference in what people say and what ze picks up emotionally. Xena has had to learn to trust hir empathic knowledge when it differs from what people are telling hir. "I have an advantage in being a sensitive person, because I have learned to trust what I feel about people and avoid those who could hurt me." But figuring it out was hard, particularly when ze was younger and less willing to compromise hir stance. Ze made a lot of mistakes because many social rules just didn't make sense to hir or seemed ridiculously complicated and unnecessary. As an adult, Xena feels ze is better at compromise, but has experienced a hard lesson learning which rules you can ignore, and which ones have to be followed to avoid trouble.

2eA people may be confused about what behaviors can get them into trouble, as social expectations are nuanced and complicated. A good friend of Xena's was accused of sexual harassment because he quoted lines from a movie sex scene to someone he liked, not understanding that most people would not respond well to this seduction effort, particularly when doing it at work. Xena knows that 2eA people are vulnerable when it comes to expressing themselves sexually. Some may have difficulty understanding the social rules about telling jokes or making sexual statements in certain situations, while others may not fully comprehend where to draw the line. Xena understands this firsthand, as ze has experienced how harsh others can be when you don't follow conventional rules of conduct.

Many of Xena's early posts about the costumes ze designed, created, and wore drew negative public attention for cultural appropriation or the wrath of homophobic trolls. Ze learned that sometimes it was not hir fault, but other times it was. Ze learned and grew from responses ze received about posts that were insensitive, offensive, or perpetuated oppressive dynamics. "I was quite naïve about my approach. I was just so excited to create these amazing costumes. I wanted to wear them and describe what they felt like in real life. I learned how to navigate social pitfalls in a very painful public way!" Cultural appropriation and policing of people in the historical costuming world is a sensitive issue. Xena became more aware and appreciative of these issues as ze matured. Ze knows there have been problems with some of the looks ze did in the past and has grown and learned a great deal from hir interactions with this community.

Over the years, Xena has had many opportunities to become informed and sensitive to the needs of other marginalized communities. Ze has been able to hone hir craft and has eventually become a role model for many other atypical people. "I've worked really hard for what I have, but I also feel lucky. I get to do what I love and be who I am. If my work helps others to get that chance, it makes it even better." Hir social media presence has given hir a robust platform for activism, as the more confident ze has become about hir message, the less worried ze was about putting it out there.

Xena's social media presence has given hir plenty of

opportunities for relationships too. Ze has had to figure out what ze needs intellectually, emotionally, and physically from potential partners. But being well known can make authentic relationships more difficult to find and sustain. Xena feels that people often have unrealistic expectations of hir, or that they believe they know hir already and don't put in the effort.

Ze has learned that some people may want to use hir for notoriety or to satisfy their own egos, to date hir just to be able to post it to social media. Xena finds it interesting to observe how much importance is placed on appearance, and how little we focus on people's true inner selves. "I feel like you can do anything with your outside shell, but what is lovable is on the inside. I know people say that it is easy for me because they think I am attractive, but they don't see what I have had to work through to be who I am."

Xena has learned how to compensate for hir sensitivities and to advocate for hirself, but it has taken time and effort to get to this level of comfort with other people. Ze has learned to protect hirself and set boundaries around hir own needs. Like many 2eA people, Xena has difficulty tolerating certain physical sensations, so has had to explore hir limits of physical love. Some activities are not tolerable for hir, such as being kissed on the mouth. Xena is turned off by kissing, and admits ze finds it a bit disgusting, due to hir particular sensitivity to others touching hir mouth. Xena has found that most of hir lovers are considerate and willing to respect hir wishes, and if they don't, ze knows that they are not right for hir.

Lawrence

Lawrence is lonely. He has never been able to sustain a long-term relationship, as the multi-dimensional needs of potential partners are difficult for him to provide for. The things he finds the most problematic are others' expectations around communication, commitment, and sex. Lawrence doesn't seem to share the same level of desire for emotional and physical connection as many of the people with whom he has met and wanted to date. He often feels disconnected from others.

By his culture's standards, he should not have difficulty finding a life partner. He is an attractive, intelligent, and successful man. He has always been gifted in understanding numbers and predicting patterns, skills that have brought him financial abundance. He has the means to own a home, travel, purchase designer goods, engage in leisure, and retire in comfort. In every way that counts in his capitalist society, Lawrence is considered a success. Yet, he feels like a failure most of the time.

Lawrence has never figured out how to mask successfully. He has a razor wit and is sarcastically funny at times, but at other times he just comes across as rude and cruel. Most people he meets don't share his obsessive love of statistics; instead they want to make small talk about current news or pop-culture events. Small talk is the main reason Lawrence hates socializing. He finds it boring but is also confused and irritated by rhetorical questions and social niceties. He interacts well with others at work, as long as they are discussing topics that are relevant to their projects. When people begin to have casual conversations, he tunes out or excuses himself. He feels like most people talk about trivial subjects, take too long to get to the point, or don't really know what they are talking about.

Lawrence doesn't hesitate to correct people who say things that are not accurate. He is blunt, brusque, and brutally honest. Before he started his own investment firm, he had difficulty with supervisors and co-workers thinking he was a self-centered jerk. His accuracy and number genius usually brought him some leeway at work, even when he made interpersonal fumbles, such as publicly calling out a co-worker for taking credit for another's work or correcting his supervisor's presentation in front of a client. Lawrence does not have the capacity to lie, even when a white lie might help him or others to save face.

He struggled both at work and at play, finding himself exhausted at the end of every day he had to interact with others. Eventually, Lawrence got tired of the relational demands of a communal work-space and started his own firm, working by himself at home. This allowed him to fully focus on his work and he was relieved to be away from people for most of the day. As he built his financial success, he was able to hire people to help him with jobs he did not have the patience or skills to do, such as administrative work and housekeeping. These employer/employee relationships worked well as long as his employees followed his instructions accurately and focused on their jobs. If they made mistakes, or tried to be social with him, Lawrence could be a harsh boss. He tried to com-pensate for his exacting standards by paying his workers well.

For the most part, he was able to retain employees for rea-sonable lengths of time, but he felt there was little he could do to sustain personal relationships. Even the most motivated po-tential love interests became discouraged by his social behaviors. A woman he dated a few times accused him of being a cold and distant intellectual snob. Another had been frustrated by what she considered his obsessive need for order and predictability. A third found him to be critical and intolerant, which she attributed to his large ego and personal certainty. Others complained about his lack of spontaneity and inability to compromise as their reasons for losing interest. Most found him to be a poor communicator who had trouble listening or adequately addressing their concerns.

Lawrence admits that all these women had legitimate com-plaints. He finds relationships difficult and confusing. Many of his reactions to women he dated were due to differences in inter-pretations of socializing and commitment. Lawrence has come to understand that his version of the world is very different from the experiences of others. For example, he is irritated by how much other people expect him to become involved in the minutiae of their own problems. He is surprised at others' attempts to engage him in conversations about everything from their recent fight with their mother to their disappointing vacation. Lawrence doesn't share this need for collaboration on everyday issues. He sees himself as an independent person who resolves his own problems and doesn't understand why others can't do the same. The last thing he would want to do is talk to other people about his personal disappointments.

He knows his unwillingness to listen to problems and provide support to others is limiting his possibilities but is equally frustrated that people don't see how difficult some of these expectations are for him. He is totally exhausted by most social events, even those that are filled with people, but don't require conversation, such as a movie or museum. Consequently, he is picky about what he subjects himself to, often opting to stay home. This reluctance to participate in many social events is hard for potential friends and lovers to accept.

The few times Lawrence has been successful at establishing a relationship, it tends to fizzle out after a few months. Due, in large part, to his disengagement from other aspects of their lives. Refusing to meet their friends at a bar, have lunch with their family, or attend their work event can erode commitment and create distance, even among those who are more introverted. One former girlfriend, who liked to stay home a great deal herself, was frustrated by his reluctance to engage in even a few outside activities with her.

In musing on his failed relationships, Lawrence acknowledges that he was often not a good companion and knows this was a disappointment to his partners. "What they didn't seem to understand was that going out and socializing was not a pleasurable activity for me. Participating in social activities takes so much energy, and the payback is nonexistent. I always hoped they would be okay with just going on their own." Lawrence wishes he was more outgoing and compatible. He knows he can be overly rational, which can detract from empathetic understanding of others' emotions. He would like to be able to find interest in the lives of others, or engage in activities that are important to them, but is also frustrated that there is little allowance and compassion for his own struggles.

Lawrence has always been confused and overwhelmed by the social norms of flirting, dating, and partnering. There are many unwritten rules and assumed knowledge within social interactions, such as holding comfortable eye contact, asking appropriate questions, participating in reciprocal conversation, and following expected levels of pacing toward intimacy. Lawrence finds that he often gets it wrong, which increases his levels of social anxiety and deflates his self-confidence. This cycle of effort and failure has impacted his willingness to keep trying to meet people and find companions.

Sometimes conversation feels incomprehensible for Lawrence too. He struggles to communicate his meaning because he doesn't always know how his words will be interpreted. For example, on a recent date, the woman asked him if he was enjoying the outing with her and he answered, "No," because he wasn't a fan of "walking through the park for no apparent reason or without a pre-determined destination." When she got angry, he tried to explain that he liked having her presence and felt they were companionable; but didn't find what she enjoyed doing to be mutually interesting. When she retorted that relationships were all about sharing interests and enjoying spending time with someone, Lawrence was genuinely puzzled that she was offended. He liked her and was trying his best to be a pleasant companion, despite not enjoying the activity. He was a bit perplexed that someone should need that level of attention and validation.

Lawrence does not think love should rely so heavily on how a person spends their time or what they find interesting and pleasurable. He believes that love is a mental and societal construct, which is not always correlated to the physical or sexual sensations he feels in his body. He is able to feel compassion and love, but not always in typical ways. For example, he often doesn't experience sexual desire until he feels he has a strong connection to his potential partner, which can be misinterpreted by others. He has struggled to understand other people's motivation and frustrations, while also feeling empathy for their disappointment. It is often hard for him to interpret what others are feeling, and to find language to describe his own feelings. He has experienced companionship in shared goals or future plans with others but doesn't rely on them for his own sense of purpose. When he does feel connection, tenderness, and companionship, he often has difficulty effectively responding to those feelings.

Lawrence also struggles with negative emotions and how they are expressed by others. He frequently misses communication through facial expressions or body language that would indicate disappointment, frustration, or anger in a more neurotypical relationship. Innuendo and non-direct communication, such as sighs or a change in tone of voice, are harder for Lawrence to decipher. He is often blindsided by another's anger toward him, as he didn't pick up on the signals leading to the outburst, so it feels sudden and disproportionate. Intense anger and shouting make him feel overwhelmed, and he usually retreats from arguments. His avoidance and withdrawal leaves others feeling that nothing is resolved. He has not been able to authentically connect with potential romantic partners in ways that felt normal or sustainable to him. He has yet to find someone who is understanding of his own struggles and willing to give him some leeway and time to figure it out with them.

Lawrence sees his rigidity, occasional withdrawal, adherence to routine, and need for intellectual stimulation as being essential to his functionality, while understanding that it presents a barrier to companionship. He knows his impatience and intolerance for the mundane have impacted his interactions with others; but they are hardwired into his mental processes. In the moment, he rarely notices how he might affect others, and is often surprised when people tell him they think he is being harsh or that his expectations are unreasonable. From his perspective, his behaviors are logical and reflect a clear view of what will work and what won't.

He has come to realize that others expect him to understand their perspective and act in ways that acknowledge their needs, and he is frustrated that this does not come naturally to him. Lawrence wishes he could be more neurotypical when it comes to relationships. He has had so many failed attempts and so much negative feedback that, at this point, he doesn't trust anyone who expresses an interest in him. He feels they are more likely to be attracted to his money. He is sad and discouraged, because he knows his past efforts have not been enough to find a partner who is a compatible equal.

Now in his 40s, Lawrence is aware he needs to change something if he is going to be able to have a relationship that lasts. He wants to find someone he can partner with to raise a family and grow old together. He feels he is missing out on a key part of life. While Lawrence is very self-aware of his own neurobiology and how to adapt his environment to meet his needs, he is still not confident in his ability to consistently meet another person's needs. He wonders if having a partner who is also 2eA would help him achieve a relationship that is more compatible and attuned. Lawrence is frustrated and discouraged but doesn't know exactly what to do to find love.

ADVICE

~ Many 2eA people struggle to develop self-awareness and may not fully understand how they impact other people. You may not be able to describe your own, or others', emotions, and have difficulty controlling your emotions. Working to build a sense of self, to create an internal autobiography, can help to increase your knowledge about yourself.

~ 2eA people may need routine and predictability and may even be rigid about their needs. This can make it difficult to acknowledge and respond to a partner's needs. Making a schedule of events to structure time and activities together can capitalize on love of routine, while making time to develop deeper bonds.

~ Set up meetings with potential dates in environments where you are comfortable and able to be at your best. For example, if you enjoy being outdoors, arrange to meet at a local park or nature trail. Being in an environment that you enjoy, or one that reduces your anxiety, will increase your ability to connect socially. Meeting someone you are interested in is stressful for everyone, so try to reduce any other stressors that can impact your functionality.

~ Find people who share one of your passions; small talk is easier when you both love to talk about the same topic.

~ Use creative ways to explore and share interests, such as fan fiction, call-in livestreams/radio, art, theater, or music appreciation/critique groups, volunteer opportunities, supper clubs, meetups, and so on.

~ Learn to advocate for yourself about the things that matter most and what you need from a friend. Equally important, learn to be less rigid on things that don't matter so much to you. Collaboration and communication are key to developing any relationship.

~ You may increase your comfort and skills around romance and intimacy a little later in life than neurotypical people. This can be due to asynchronous development, or from lack of opportunity, but many 2eA people are able to develop satisfying relationships over time.

~ Be aware of your pacing. Consider where your potential partner is in moving the relationship forward and try to match that. Sometimes 2eA people misread social cues and may try to move deeper into the relationship too quickly. On the other hand, they may miss clues that their potential partner is interested and ready for more and hold back unnecessarily. When in doubt, ask questions to find out how your partner feels and what they want.

~ You may not have had adequate opportunities to develop relationships when you were growing up, or you may not have felt you had peers who were similar to yourself. This can lead to bouts of social anxiety, which makes it difficult to feel competent and be comfortable with typical adult socializing, such as meeting new people, expressing interest in getting to know someone better, or suggesting a shared activity. You may have to learn these skills with the help of a therapist or social support group. Look for people who have expertise in 2eA issues, or at the very least, in working with atypical people.

~ It is not unusual for 2eA people to have been taken advantage of socially, often from childhood on. While some are highly socially adept, others may be gullible or naïve when it comes to social norms and expectations. Unfortunately, this can lead to situations that are not equitable, healthy, or enjoyable. If you find yourself in a group where you always pay for everyone's dinner or spend a great deal of time driving a friend to their events or appointments, take a moment to analyze how this is impacting your own life. If you don't enjoy driving the friend, or find you are financially impacted by social events, practice saying "No." You can tell people you will get back to them on any request that puts you on the spot. Often, deferring an answer gives you time to analyze the impact of the request, and decide whether or not it could work for you. Putting off answering until later allows you to say "No" from a time and place where you feel safer, such as texting them once you get home.

~ You can do some self-help exercises for social anxiety, such as identifying areas of challenge and practicing small, safe ways to address your fears. For example, if you are nervous speaking to people you don't know, or may have just met, you can practice saying a friendly comment to the server as you order your coffee or compliment someone standing with you at the bus stop. Some 2eA people will be better at social language than others, so if thinking of compliments or friendly comments does not come easily to you, do some research online or get help from a trusted person. Anticipating problems and exploring solutions, as well as debriefing with a trusted person when something goes wrong, can also help to build confidence.

~ Many 2eA people are perfectionists and may experience intolerance for the imperfections of others. If you find yourself being rigid about how others interact with you, it can help to analyze your areas of inflexibility. Perfectionism is related to anxiety and can be addressed through anxiety-centered therapies like CBT.

~ Self-compassion is the foundation for friendship, as it is difficult to believe that others like/love you if you don't like/love yourself. Self-care is the next step in building relationships; you need to know what makes you feel safe, comfortable, and cared for before you can tell others what you need in a relationship. It is important to identify your own dis/abilities and stressors to be able to create environments that help reduce those issues, such as compensating for auditory-processing issues by meeting friends at a quiet museum instead of a noisy cafe. It is much easier to be your authentic self with others if you know when and where to socialize for optimum engagement.

~ 2eA people might put others off with their approach, as they are often direct and may not like small talk. They may also find that their own emotions/actions might be out of sync with others in the room. Making efforts to observe how others are acting, and adjusting your own actions, can make it easier to make initial connections. Once you have met people and begun to establish a relationship, helping others to understand your thought processes and social patterns may increase their willingness to support your efforts.

~ All humans have differing levels of intuition and empathy, but 2eA people may have sensitivity levels that are higher than neurotypical people. Trusting your own intuition may help you avoid situations that could be difficult or dangerous.

~ 2eA people often develop their social, emotional, and intellectual abilities in asynchronous ways. Be kind to yourself if you are slower to obtain skills in social or emotional developmental areas, your brain is built that way. Building skills may be slower for you in some ways, and you may only be able to create change incrementally.

~ Others may have differing levels of commitment based on their own circumstances. 2eA people may be out-of-sync with neurotypical peers in their timing or commitment, but it can be difficult to read the other person's social signals. If possible, learning to read facial expression, body language, and tone of voice can help to improve your ability to understand another's interest or readiness for various steps in relational growth. This will help you to be more in sync with your partner's needs.

~ As a dis/abled person, you may experience discrimination and an imbalance of power in a relationship. Being able to advocate for yourself, knowing your innate worth, and setting healthy boundaries are all necessary for building fulfilling relationships. For some 2eA people, keeping or repairing relationships may have been areas of challenge their entire lives, and they may have deep wounds from those experiences. This may make it difficult for them to collaborate and communicate effectively. For example, if you are a person who has difficulty expressing your feelings when you are upset, set a framework for communication that gives you time and support to state your needs when you are calm and functional. This can be done by using postponement statements like "I need a minute, I will come back when I feel ready," or "Can we talk about this when we are both calm?"

~ Many 2eA people have been told that they are the problem their entire lives, and you may be sensitive to criticism. Help your friends and partners to learn to clearly state what they need/want from you using "I" messages (such as "I feel like you care about me when you do…"), rather than using accusations or disparagement.

~ Be honest about your tolerance levels when expressing/receiving physical affection. You have a right to express love and desire in ways that are authentic and pleasurable for you. Physical aspects of being 2eA may create levels of difficulty with sensory triggers and overexcitabilities. 2eA people may also have to work harder at understanding and accepting their sexual self, which can impact the development of sexual socialization skills. Communicate with your partner to establish what each person needs and be accepting and respectful of each other. Some people are better at nonverbal communication, flirting, sexual language, and expressing desire than others. Explore ways to connect and accommodate each other's needs in ways that are mutually acceptable.

~ Humans are wired for love and connection, but we learn to have relationships through our relationships. Many 2eA people have not had secure attachment and positive relationships throughout their lives, so may have to learn how to be a friend or partner as an adult. It helps to teach others about 2eA culture and be an advocate for yourself and your community, as people may be more empathetic and understanding if they understand your history and challenges.

~ Many 2eA persons are nonconformists who resist societal pressures to change their behaviors, and this can lead to relational problems if your love interest does not share your nonconformist values. You can work to find compromises that foster relationships with those outside your culture, or you may prefer to start with those who are also 2eA. Either way, you have the right to find love, sexual fulfillment, and lasting partnerships that honor your individuality.

Partnerships and Family Life

P ARTNERING WITH 2EA PEOPLE can be complex and bewildering, particularly if you are neurotypical. For 2eA people, overexcitabilities, difficulty with emotional attachment, lack of attunement, and low tolerance for the mundane can derail relationships and make forming a family an unreachable goal. When you are a 2eA person, the expectations of others can also be a barrier to family life. What if you are asexual or polyamorous? What if you crave partnership but are intensely private? How do you find acceptance for creating a new way of partnering?

Anna

Anna never felt good about herself growing up. She was a poor student throughout her schooling and ended up dropping out of college. She had difficulty maintaining friendships and was pretty lonely during her school years. Anna didn't understand why learning and socializing was more difficult for her until she completed a neuropsychological evaluation and received her autism spectrum disorder, sensory-processing disorder, and gifted diagnoses as an adult. She now understands why school was always such a challenge and why life felt so hard.

Anna's psychologist was not fully familiar with 2eA characteristics and challenges, so missed some things in her evaluation. For example, Anna is a highly sensitive person[1] (HSP) who is extremely impacted by both external and internal states. She is exhausted by most social interactions and by loud, busy environments. She experiences sensory input intensely and may become overwhelmed by smells, sounds, visual movement, and being bumped by others.

Additionally, she is strongly impacted by her internal functions, such as when she is hungry, has a full bladder, or is sick. She is also keenly aware of where her body is within her physical space and its minute interactions within the environment. She can't tolerate clothing that is tight or uncomfortable and certain textures make her skin crawl.

When Anna feels social pressure and judgment, her sensitivities increase and her ability to process conversation or respond appropriately is diminished. She can also become confused and disoriented in large public spaces and has had panic attacks if she feels lost. Anna has been ashamed of herself for most of her life, as she sees her inability to function "normally" as a personal failure.

After learning about her diagnoses, Anna spent a year doing intense research on her dis/abilities to develop a better understanding of her needs. This allowed her to release some of her shame about her perceived failures and to begin to develop strategies. Over time, Anna was able to figure out how to calm herself in social situations by reducing other stressors. For example, if she knew she would be attending a party, she would eat and use the bathroom before she left home. She would also ensure she had on comfortable clothing and carried a smooth stone in her pocket that she could rub to reduce anxiety. Anna also learned how to recognize the

---

1   HSPs experience acute physical, mental, or emotional responses to stimuli. For more on HSPs, read *The Highly Sensitive Person: How to Thrive When the World Overwhelms You* by Dr. Elaine Aron (1997).

signs that she was becoming overstimulated and excuse herself to find a quiet spot. In a place where the stimuli was reduced, Anna's nervous system could calm down and allow her to recover before returning to the party.

Anna has also learned to set boundaries around what events she will attend, and to give herself permission to cancel if she is not feeling strong and capable. Eventually, Anna's coping strategies allowed her to increase her social skills and comfort level to the point she felt ready to try to get a job. She found an entry-level job at a large tech company as a proofreader. Anna is an excellent, fast reader who is able to easily pick out details that others might miss. She was very good at her job, and because it was easy for her, she could focus her energy on other aspects of the work environment that were more taxing.

Anna found that some of her co-workers shared similar dis/abilities, one had ADHD and another struggled with anxiety, and most of the people in the office were understanding and accommodating. Through work, she eventually met and fell in love with the man who is now her husband, Geoff. "He is a lot like me, which is both a blessing and a curse. We have the same type of relational weaknesses, we are both a little rigid, easily overstimulated, and unable to let go of issues. But we also share the same sense of humor, love of quiet evenings at home, and are sexually compatible. We have been able to figure out how to be a couple and enjoy each other's company."

Anna and Geoff worked through how to resolve arguments, collaborate on life decisions, and build a trusting bond. They found ways to compromise on some of the bigger issues couples face, like combining finances and setting up a home together, without too many arguments. They were able to discuss options and collaborate on when to start a family. Once they started trying, Anna got pregnant right away. They were excited about becoming parents and started planning for the arrival of the baby. Since Geoff earned a good income, they decided that Anna would be the primary stay-at-home caregiver.

Anna wanted to make sure she researched how to assemble a supportive birthing team who could understand her sensitivities and help her through the birth experience. She was able to find a doula, Stephanie, who specialized in supporting neurodiverse clients. Stephanie would help Anna know what to expect, particularly related to her sensory issues, as well as advocating for her during the birth. Anna was very specific and particular about trying to put systems in place that would help her cope.

At that point, Geoff deferred to Anna on all decisions about preparing for the baby's arrival. "It made it easier. Geoff was supportive but hands-off, which was great when we were preparing for the baby, but less great once Cyrell arrived." Geoff also stepped back during the birth. He was able to be an emotional support to Anna but was happy that Stephanie took care of all the advocacy and practical responsibilities. He felt he was out of his comfort zone when it came to birth and babies.

After the baby was born, Anna saw that Geoff was also squeamish about taking care of Cyrell's physical needs. He was grossed out by spit up and poopy diapers, both types of messes that babies create on a regular basis. While she also struggled with sensory issues, Anna was able to attend to Cyrell without feeling too overwhelmed most days. Geoff tried to support Anna in other ways and helped with the cleaning and cooking when he got home from work each evening.

One of the things Anna found hardest about being a mother was the relentless need to be attentive to the baby's needs. She expected that her sleep and free time would be impacted when she had her baby, but she was surprised at how much work she had to do every day. There was very little respite from the monotony of her days, and she often felt tense and reactive. Geoff was worried about her and tried to do whatever he could to give her a break once he got home from work. Eventually, Geoff and Anna settled into a routine, and that helped things feel more stable and manageable.

As Cyrell grew, Geoff was able to be more involved and often took him for walks in the evening to give Anna time to herself. Anna found she needed to spend most evenings trying to catch up on everything she was unable to do during her days with Cyrell. Anna loved being a mom, but she missed being able to spend an evening reading or going for a solitary bike ride. Anna also missed time with Geoff, as their lives were now focused on being parents.

While they were not planning on having another baby so soon, and despite birth-control efforts, Anna realized she was pregnant again. She was unsure how she felt about this news, as she worried that she might not be able to handle having a second child. "I felt like I was just learning how to be a mom, never mind trying to keep up with all the housework. All those old feelings of shame washed over me because I knew plenty of women who had multiple kids and seemed to handle it just fine. Motherhood started to feel like another area in my life where I was going to be a failure."

After Pru was born, Anna struggled to stay on top of caring for a new baby, a toddler, and a home. Even though this is true for many women, Anna felt she was particularly challenged in meeting those expectations. She began to have panic attacks if too many things were going wrong at once. Geoff took time off work to help when he could, but Anna began to feel her life was spinning out of control.

Anna's Mom came to stay with them to take care of the children and the housework to give Anna some relief. Her efforts to help Anna get organized and develop routines just made Anna feel less and less capable. She was embarrassed and felt her Mom saw her as incompetent. "I know she loves me and was trying to help, but it always felt like she was criticizing me. I began to experience a stupid resurgence of teenage rebellion, which made things harder between my Mom and me."

Anna eventually started to see a psychologist, Dr. Ricki, who specialized in working with autistic adults. Dr. Ricki was able to help Anna better understand the impact of being a HSP, as well as the more nuanced aspects of being a gifted person with autism and anxiety. They explored her feelings about her relationship with her own mother and how her lack of understanding about autism had created hardship for both of them.

Dr. Ricki helped Anna to work through past traumas and develop self-compassion. Anna learned about the importance of providing her children with attention and care when they needed it, to give them secure attachment. Anna wanted her children to have good self-esteem, but it is hard to pass that along if you can't love yourself. Anna's work with Dr. Ricki helped her to recognize her own worth and feel more capable and accepting of her own style of mothering. Anna learned to be the kind of mom she wanted to be, while also recognizing and taking care of her own needs.

She began to understand how all of the sensory and emotional pressures created burnout. Dr. Ricki and Anna worked on recognizing how the increased stressors of parenting had incrementally destabilized Anna's previously developed systems of work and self-care. Anna began to analyze each aspect of her life that contributed to her burnout and address them with Dr. Ricki. She also helped Anna develop routines and practical strategies for childcare and homekeeping. Eventually, as Anna began to feel she had more control over her days, her anxiety lessened.

Dr. Ricki also helped Anna to recognize and be attuned to her needs in her relationship. She is getting better at communicating with Geoff, to clearly state her needs, including giving him lists of what she wants him to do each week. He appreciates her direct, concrete statements and lists because they remove ambiguity. Anna and Geoff also give each other time to pursue solitary activities, as they know that both of them need time alone. Geoff has become better at checking in with Anna each day and working together to tackle problems.

Anna has cultivated regular routines, such as getting up at the same time each morning and setting her schedule of tasks for the day, including making time to do something for herself that makes her happy. These routines allow her to do what needs to be done each day, while still making time to nurture her authentic self.

Her trauma work with Dr. Ricki has also begun to address the inherent sexism in her cultural norms, and to empower Anna to advocate for herself. "I finally began to get angry at all the ridiculous expectations society puts on moms. We are supposed to be able to meet all our children's needs, keep your house running, ensure kids are fed, and be a good partner. And if you also have a career, you are supposed to be great at that too. It is not a sustainable system and I have learned not to care what others think."

Anna and Geoff have developed systems that work for them, while respecting healthy self-care boundaries. "We have a *no judgment* rule at home. If we eat frozen dinners for a week, or the kids are wearing the last clean thing in the drawer, it's okay. We take time for relaxation, having fun, and being kind to each other. If we are stressed, we hide at home all day in our pj's and focus on comfort. Our family's values are different from the mainstream in some ways, but they work for all of us."

Anna and Geoff will likely need to recalibrate their systems as their children grow and begin to integrate into the larger community. While Cyrell and Pru have not yet been diagnosed, Anna can see echoes of Geoff and herself in them. Anna and Geoff want to do what they can to proactively address the common problems 2eA children may encounter. They know they may need to advocate for their children at school, or even find alternative educational methods, if school is not working. Geoff and Anna are motivated to help their children be proud of who they are and hope to prevent the feelings of shame and failure that they felt when they were children.

They are going to work to help others fully understand their children's behavior. Too often, 2eA children are judged and punished for behaviors that are a response to the environment or simply who they are. They may act out if they are anxious or bored, and most teachers are not trained to recognize and respond appropriately to behaviors that are related to 2eA issues. Anna and Geoff have become more aware of their own needs and responses to stressors, so will likely be able to help their children more effectively. Having medical, therapeutic, and academic professionals who truly understand the needs of 2eA people can be life-changing. It can mean the difference between growing up feeling that there is something wrong with you, and growing up understanding you are part of a valid culture.

Sam

Etta and Sam have a blended family. Sam had a child of her own prior to her relationship with Etta, and is currently pregnant with her second child, their first as a couple. Sam left her husband to partner with Etta, but he is still very much a part of their lives. Sam has created a different life for her children compared to her own childhood experiences. However, it took her many years to figure out who she was and what she needed in a relationship.

Sam's parents were conservative, wealthy, and exacting. They had high standards for their children and expected them to adopt their family values and fit into their community. Sam never felt like she belonged in her family, though she spent her childhood trying her best to please her parents and conform to their expectations. This was difficult for Sam, as she was not good at being the type of girl her Mom expected her to be.

She was never popular in school, despite having brothers who were. Her Mom tried to arrange playdates and foster friendships with her classmates when she was younger but gave up by the time Sam was in middle school. Sam remembers her Mom's embarrassment and frustration when no one attended her carefully planned 7-year-old birthday party. Her Mom told Sam that this was the result of not trying hard enough to make and keep friends. She was exasperated with Sam's lack of enthusiasm and told her she didn't understand how her only daughter could be so different from herself. Sam felt deeply ashamed that she wasn't the daughter her mother wanted.

She was also hard on herself for not having a better understanding of what to do to be popular. Sam felt she was lacking some key component in being able to understand and carry out social interactions. She wanted to have friends, but she just couldn't find anyone she felt she could relate to or who shared her interests. Her Mom told her she came across as a know-it-all, and that turned other kids off. She urged Sam to stop talking about topics that other kids found boring. This made Sam sad, as one of the things she loved was talking about her interests.

As Sam's social difficulties became more pronounced, her Mom made an appointment for her to see a psychologist. She hoped that they might find a way to teach Sam to be more socially in-tune. When the psychologist told Sam's Mom that he believed Sam was on the autism spectrum and recommended testing, the visits to the psychologist promptly ended. Sam felt a distinct difference in how her Mom interacted with her after that. There was much less focus on trying to get Sam to be more socially successful. Her Mom stopped arranging play dates and parties, which was a relief for Sam but also painful, as she felt she had failed her Mom in some fundamental way.

Sam continued to try to please her parents the only way she could, through being a perfect student. She always earned straight A's and excelled in every academic endeavor but didn't enjoy much about school until she started high school. There she could take advanced placement classes that gave her an opportunity to work at an accelerated pace. Her teachers were surprised at how much she already knew, and some began to give her even more advanced work. Sam was particularly good at science and math and took as many accelerated classes as she could in those areas. Her parents began to be less critical of her lack of social skills and focus more on her academic prowess. They were pleased and proud when she graduated high school with the highest honors.

Sam decided to pursue a degree in biochemistry and was accepted into a prestigious university. She passed all her entrance exams with nearly perfect scores, so was able to take more advanced courses right from the start. She enjoyed the academic rigor and felt that she was finally able to fully engage her mind. Even though she didn't like dorm life, Sam was also relieved to live away from home. For the first time, she felt free from the pressure to be socially active. Sam threw her energies into her work, often taking more courses per semester than were required. She was excited to take highly advanced classes and reveled in reading the latest scientific research for her assignments. By the time she completed her undergraduate degree, Sam decided she wanted to be a doctor.

Sam's prodigious memory allowed her to score in the top percentage on her medical college admissions exams and she was accepted into a highly regarded medical school known for their research program. The harder she had to work the happier Sam became. Not only because she could fully engage her intellect, but also because there were no expectations to engage in social activities. As a medical student, everyone expected her to be too busy to socialize, and even when she was home, her parents deferred to her need to rest. Sam was also relieved by her Mom's newly adjusted attention to her education, rather than on her appearance or social life.

As Sam progressed through her residency, she knew she wanted to focus on research. Her abilities and interest were noted by one of the supervising doctors, Jocelyne, and she recommended Sam for a fellowship in research. Over the years, Jocelyne became Sam's mentor and Sam blossomed under her tutelage. Sam felt she had finally found someone who truly understood and accepted her. As a gifted person, Jocelyne was Sam's intellectual peer and didn't expect her to engage in small talk or other social activities that Sam found to be a waste of time. Jocelyne supported Sam throughout her schooling and eventually helped her find a position at the end of her fellowship.

Sam joined a research team who were working on genomic medicine, which she found fascinating. Sam began to feel she had found her place in the world, as most of her colleagues had similar interests and intellect. Being surrounded by people like her, Sam began to enjoy her time with her fellow researchers, and her confidence in herself grew. When she met Mark, a newly hired team member, she felt a connection. He was passionate about their research and focused on things Sam found meaningful. His brain seemed to process data the way hers did and they shared a similar work ethic. As Sam and Mark began to spend more time together, they found a growing sense of comfort in each other's company. Over the next year, they spent increasing time together and their relationship blossomed.

One of the things that Sam appreciated about Mark was his independence. He was happy to give her space when she needed it and never pressured her to join him in outings. Mark was happy that Sam had no problem with his going out to meet friends and never criticized his activities. They could spend quality time together but were also comfortable with spending time apart. Their lives seemed compatible.

As their commitment to each other grew, Mark proposed to Sam. Her parents were excited about the engagement, as Mark was from a similar background and they felt he was a great match for their daughter. Sam was very busy with work, and not all that interested in the wedding itself, so let her Mom and Mark plan the details. The first clue that there might be difficulties in their partnership came as the wedding plans emerged. Her Mom wanted a large and extravagant wedding and pressured Mark to follow her lead. When Sam complained to Mark, he told her it was important to their families and promised he would help her through it. Sam didn't want to be difficult, so agreed to go along with the plan. Despite discomfort with most of the activities and requirements of the day, Sam managed to get through it and was relieved to put the event behind her.

After their honeymoon, Mark and Sam moved into an

apartment together near their research facility and began setting up house and developing shared routines. While they had often stayed over at each other's apartments before they married, they found it was a different experience to combine their households. Sam and Mark had tried to blend their furnishings and decor, but Mark was a collector who liked to display his prized items. These displays made Sam feel visually exhausted and she sometimes needed to retreat to the spare bedroom to escape from sensory overload. Mark appreciated Sam's preference for minimalist décor and tried to keep his collections to just a few areas of their home, but he missed the overstuffed feeling of his own apartment. They wanted to figure out a way to make their home work for both of them and tried to be collaborative in their decisions.

They also worked to appreciate each other's interests and attend to their individual needs. Sam liked Mark's friends and occasionally participated in their outings, even though she sometimes had to work hard to attend to conversations and join in activities. Mark was an extrovert, but he understood Sam's need for more downtime. He tried to spend a few evenings a week at home with just the two of them, but Sam was not always a good conversationalist after a long day at work. She used all of her energy to be engaged with people at work and had little interest in more conversation once she got home. Mark unwound through cooking and engaging in discussions, so he often felt a bit impatient with their time together. Despite their efforts to accommodate each other, Sam began to feel overwhelmed and exhausted by the increased social interactions, while Mark became frustrated with how much more quiet time at home that Sam needed to decompress.

They did their best to be a couple and enjoyed many aspects of their relationship. They stuck with established routines and generally found ways to cooperate with each other. Then Mark began to talk about starting a family. They had discussed having children when they were dating but hadn't revisited the idea much since their wedding. Sam also wanted children but wasn't sure about the timing. Mark worried about postponing the decision for too long, as he was in his 40s and wanted to have children now so he could be active and healthy while they were growing up.

Sam felt she was ready in many ways but wanted to make sure she was emotionally capable of motherhood. She was determined to figure out how to raise her child in a more positive and nurturing environment than she had experienced, long before she ever made it a reality. Sam decided to see a therapist to try to work through some of her issues with her mother and address her worries about becoming a mom. Through her work with her new therapist, Jeni, she was able to begin to see how her parents' distant, judgmental, and often harsh methods throughout her childhood had impacted her other relationships. Jeni also diagnosed Sam's autism and giftedness and helped her to understand how that impacted her everyday life. They reviewed what created the most stress for Sam, like social pressures, and what helped her feel calmer, such as being surrounded by order and solitude. Jeni also helped Sam to recognize that in many situations there is an inherent bias against women, particularly those with dis/abilities. Sam began to feel that some of Mark's expectations and attitudes toward her were ableist. Jeni helped Sam to begin to do some self-reflection and identify how to align her actions with what she valued in life.

Eventually, Sam began to be able to set boundaries with Mark and stand up for what she needed from their relationship, and that helped her to feel more ready to have a baby. She and Mark decided to try that spring, and Sam was pregnant by the end of the year. To help her feel more confident, Sam took some parenting classes and read books on what to expect in the first few years of her baby's life.

She knew her perfectionism and anxiety often created situations where she took things to the extreme. She also thought that she might not react well to the sensory onslaught of parenting. Sam was sure that she would need help but wasn't as certain in Mark's ability to be an equal partner in parenting. Mark was raised with the notion that you hired someone to help with the day-to-day parenting tasks when your children were young. He felt his responsibilities and interaction with his children would come when they were school-aged. He could picture himself taking them to places on the weekend or teaching them to play baseball once they grew. Babies seemed to need connection and care he could not provide.

Sam also felt that babies needed expert care but wanted to be a different kind of mother than either her own or Mark's mother had been. Sam also loved her career and wanted to continue to work half time after the baby was born. She spent the last few months of her pregnancy finding someone she felt she could trust with her baby. She hired Yori, an experienced nanny who had worked with several families and had successfully raised her own children.

When Sam's daughter, Joy, was born, Yori became Sam's lifeline. Yori took care of Joy as if she were her own baby and graciously helped Sam to feel confident in caring for an infant. Mark appreciated Yori's competent care of his daughter and was happy to avoid the day-to-day needs of a baby. As Joy grew, Yori and Sam became the primary people in her life. Even though he loved his baby girl, Mark didn't spend a great deal of time with her. Mark had grown up in a household where cleaning and childcare jobs were done by employees, which gave the adults more leisure time. But Sam didn't seem to take advantage of that adult time. When she got home from work, she was devoted to spending time with Joy or finding a bit of the quiet time she craved. Mark felt increasingly disconnected from Sam.

He also knew that just being in the house sometimes intruded into Sam's quiet time, so he began to spend more of his free time with friends. Sam wanted Mark to be more connected to Joy but tried to understand his perspective. She also grew up in a house where nannies were the primary caregivers for the children, but she didn't want that for Joy. She saw echoes of her own parents in Mark's approach to parenting and felt he was missing out on Joy's infancy. Mark resented Sam's attentions to the baby and thought she was being unreasonable in how focused she was on Joy. He thought she should still make time for doing other things. Mark tried to convince Sam to get out more and do things for herself. He also reassured her that he would be more involved when Joy was a little older. Their frustration over their parenting differences often resulted in arguments, so Mark began to spend even less time at home, and Sam retreated even further.

Shortly after Joy's first birthday, Mark told Sam he felt their marriage wasn't really working for him. He suggested they separate for a while to give each other a break and see if it helped release some of the tension between them. Sam agreed to the separation, as she also felt their relationship was strained, and Mark was already spending most of his time away from home anyway.

Mark moved into his own apartment but tried to come by each week to spend some time with them. Sam found that after Mark moved out, she was able to set predictable routines and create a more peaceful atmosphere at home. Sam was much less tense because she could focus more of her energy on caring for Joy and for herself. As Joy grew into toddlerhood, Sam and Mark decided to establish a consistent routine so Joy could see her Dad every weekend. They often planned family outings that gave them some joint parenting time with Joy.

By the time Joy was in preschool, Sam and Mark had developed a system that worked fairly well for everyone. They found that living apart was good for their partnership, as they could now appreciate each other as friends. They were in agreement on most of the decisions about Joy and felt they had figured out a reasonable way to support each other as partners.

When a major research project she had been heading was completed, Sam decided to take a much-needed break. She made a plan to spend the summer in the mountains. She talked over her decision with Mark, and he thought it was a good idea. He promised to keep his regular weekend visit schedule as much as possible while they were there. Then Sam checked in with Yori to see if she would be willing to spend the summer at a mountain resort with her and Joy. With all the necessary plans in place, they headed for the mountains. It turned out to be a life-changing trip for Sam.

Etta worked as a wellness coach at the resort. She was renowned for helping guests to find ways to develop calming habits and improve their life balance. Knowing she needed to find ways to reduce stress, Sam signed up for her sunrise hike program. Once she got used to the early morning wake-up call, Sam began to enjoy the peaceful early morning walks in the forest. She found Etta to be a genuinely kind person who was interested in Sam's needs, and in helping her feel connected and grounded.

Etta was one of those people who naturally draws others to her. She is a very grounded, self-assured, easy-going person. She likes people and can generally find the good in others. After working on a cruise line and traveling the world for several years, she took the job at the mountain retreat to be closer to nature and live a more balanced life. Etta was not looking for a relationship, and the last thing she expected was to fall in love with a guest at the resort.

Etta was first attracted to Sam's unique looks. While Sam would not be considered beautiful in the conventional sense, there was something about her features that were elegant and classic. Etta tried hard not to give off any signals to Sam. She didn't know if Sam was interested, and also worried that Sam was a guest and she was an employee. Etta found herself spending a good deal of their hikes talking with Sam. She enjoyed having deep, philosophical discussions with Sam and felt they cared about many of the same things. She also liked the look that came over Sam's face when Sam talked about Joy. Etta could see that Sam was a loving mom and gentle person.

By the end of the first month, Sam realized she was attracted to Etta in ways she had not felt before. She woke up each morning looking forward to being with Etta, and when she saw her it made Sam happy. She often felt a hum of desire when she looked at Etta. Sam had not thought she was bisexual; yet, she found herself daydreaming about Etta and was surprised by the strength of her attraction. This was new for Sam, as her sex drive had always seemed to be lower than Mark's, but she was much more excited by Etta than she had ever been with Mark. However, her feelings were not just sexual, as she was also attracted to Etta's personality and outlook on life. She loved that Etta seemed to understand and appreciate her deeper feelings and felt they could connect at a spiritual level.

By the end of the summer, it was clear that their attraction was more than a casual encounter. Etta and Sam became inseparable, spending time together whenever Etta was not working. Sam decided to stay in the mountains and rented a home a few miles from the resort. Mark was a bit surprised, but also supportive, as he could continue to see Joy on the weekends and looked forward to coming to the mountains to visit his daughter. Yori agreed to move with Sam and Joy, and by early fall they were settled into their new home. Most of Sam's work could be done remotely, but she lived close enough to travel to the research facility when she needed to be onsite. She loved the drive back from the city into the calm of the mountains. She realized how tightly wound she had been for most of her life and living here allowed her to begin to let down her guard. Sam felt like she had finally come home.

As her relationship with Etta deepened, Sam told Mark she was in love with Etta and wanted a divorce. Mark was somewhat stunned by this revelation but could see the difference in Sam's demeanor. He was happy that she had found a new level of peace and contentment, and a partnership that seemed to work. Mark agreed to an amicable parting and they were able to remain friends as they ended their marriage.

The following year, Etta moved into Sam's house and they began to form their blended family. Etta tried to be informed about Sam's dis/abilities and paid attention to what Sam told her she could do to support her needs. This made Sam feel cared for and special. She believes she has found the love of her life. The bond she shares with Etta is profound for her, as she feels truly seen and accepted for the first time in her life. Etta has a deep understanding of Sam's sensitivity, intellect, and need for calm solitude. Sam is enthusiastically supportive of Etta's connection to nature and her intentional approach to caring for people and the planet.

They are respectful of each other's wants and needs and trust each other to be an equal partner in building their life together. It is a complementary coupling, as they are able to collaborate well, even when working through difficult issues around their relationship or in parenting Joy. Mark has been folded into their family, and their compatibility has enhanced his role as a third parent, albeit a less active one. He regularly visits them and has developed a genuine friendship with Etta. When Sam and Etta decided to have another baby, they asked Mark to be the biological father. Mark was happy to agree. He loves his children and feels he can be a better father in this third parent role.

Sam is grateful for the authenticity of her new lifestyle and family. She knows that her parents don't understand her relationship with Etta and Mark and are not always supportive or kind. But she doesn't feel like an outsider anymore and is not vulnerable to her parents' criticism. Etta's love and compassion have given Sam the strength to fully embrace herself and accept her unique characteristics. "Looking back at my upbringing, it is no wonder I felt out of place. I am a highly sensitive, autistic, gay woman. I don't think I knew anyone who was autistic growing up, and only one person who was gay. I want my children to grow up in a much more diverse and inclusive community. Etta, Mark, and I have worked hard to build the kind of supportive, loving family that I wish I could have had."

ADVICE

Relationships can be both rewarding and difficult for everyone, but being 2eA can add another layer of complication. From trying to find a partner to figuring out how to solidify the relationship, some aspects of partnering can be confusing for 2eA people.

~ It can be helpful to learn about relational stages and social norms to understand the pacing of typical partnerships. For example, a structure like Knapp's Relational Stages (Knapp, 1978) can help you identify the typical stages of coming together (initiating, experimenting, intensifying, integrating, bonding), or typical signs of a relationship coming apart (differentiating, circumscribing, stagnating, avoiding, terminating), and what behaviors are normally expected at each stage. There may be aspects of these stages that are more challenging for 2eA people to navigate. In the coming together stages, 2eA challenges are:

» Initiation—feeling socially different, having social anxiety, being unsure of how to meet people

» Experimentation—oversharing personal information, unskilled at small talk, struggling with relationship building

» Intensification—unable or unwilling to engage in emotional attachment

» Integration/Bonding—misreading signals, lack of attunement, low frustration tolerance, timing of stages (insecurity, need, disconnection), and asynchronous levels of intensity.

It can be equally difficult to experience the relationship coming apart:

» Differentiating—unable to recognize partner's growing individualization and separation

» Circumscribing—difficulty with arguing or expressing feelings in constructive ways

» Stagnation—partner may reach this stage without the 2eA person being aware of how it happened

» Avoidance—2eA people may not be comfortable with arguing and unintentionally push the relationship to come apart

» Terminating—it can be difficult for some 2eA people to understand how the relationship disintegrated and it may come as a surprise when a partner ends the relationship.

~ Many young adult 2eA people need a longer time to feel ready to participate in a partnership or think about starting their own family. Due to asynchronous development, it may take some years for your social/emotional maturity to catch up to your intellectual maturity. Give yourself the time you need to mature and find what works for you before you settle down or decide to have children.

~ It is also fine to remain single, or to define relationships in new and different ways. If you find partners who share your interests, are excited by the same things, and want what you want in life, don't hesitate to find a way to make it work. You might discover that you are compatible with being asexual, polyamorous, or kink. Love is love in all its glorious and complicated forms. Be open to finding what works for you.

~ Practice staying-together strategies—building communication skills, learning to tolerate difficult affective experiences, increasing empathy, building healthy attachment, developing flexibility, setting boundaries, developing intimacy, reducing defensiveness, learning to argue (timing, processing, mind-reading expectations, defensiveness, transition time, not multitasking during conversations, and concrete communication about needs) (Myhill & Jekel, 2015).

~ The most critical aspect of successful relationships for 2eA people is feeling they can safely be their authentic selves. Many have experienced insecure attachment, trauma, and internalized shame throughout their childhoods. Trying to be yourself when you have been perpetually misunderstood or maligned can be a struggle. Most of society's rules are designed to create conformity; and when society is afraid of differences, they tend to shame the outliers.

In order to have relationships that work well, partners need to understand the historical stressors and formative experiences of 2eA people.

~ There are several things 2eA people can do to build resilience within their relationships and families:

» Understand your neurodiversity. What are your gifts and dis/abilities? How does each impact your life?

» Learn to code-switch and find ways to have control over your behavior in various situations.

» Build family and friend relationships that allow you to feel you have support during times of crisis.

» Find balance and ways to meet each family member's needs.

» Hold on to your sense of what you need to thrive. "Normal" is a social construct and can be dismantled with a more neurodivergent approach.

» Work on being flexible and willing to see things from another's point of view.

» Keep a sense of hope and positivity.

» Find others who share your culture, your belief system, and your values.

~ Relationships tend to work better if everyone involved practices the following habits:

» Examine beliefs, actions, emotions. Are you doing something because you think that is what is expected, or because it resonates with you? We all need to develop our own belief system and align our actions to our feelings and beliefs.

» Recognize hidden emotions. Many 2eA people have suppressed their emotions because they have been told from a very young age that they were too sensitive, too reactive, too loud, or too exuberant. As an adult, you may have to re-examine these negative judgments and narratives about yourself and reconnect to your inner self.

» Build self-knowledge. Knowledge is power, and having a deep self-knowing can build confidence, create safety, mitigate dis/abilities and triggers, help you to negotiate difficulties, and clear a path for what you want to achieve.

» Embrace differences. As part of your inner exploration and knowledge-building, you should work toward loving your differences and authentic individuality. It is also important to find your people. There is a growing recognition of 2eA as a valid cultural expression, and inclusion in your community can be very affirming.

~ Person-centered then partner-centered actions—once you believe you are a valuable human and contributing member of your community, you can begin to expand your growth to relational success with a chosen partner. Whether your partner is also 2eA, or more neurotypical, positive communication and collaboration will build mutual respect and understanding.

~ Practice attachment. Secure attachment may be a new experience for many 2eA people, and you may need therapeutic support to heal attachment wounds, particularly if you were neglected or abused.[2] If trauma or neglect has impacted your attachment, there are excellent therapies that can help you heal and build healthy relationships.

~ Discuss and make accommodations with your partner. This is the next step in attachment, to be able to set appropriate boundaries for self and partner care. You have the right to unapologetically ask

---

2   You can self-screen using the online Adverse Childhood Experiences screening tool at sites such as https://acestoohigh.com/got-your-ace-score.

for support and accommodation of your needs. There should be equity and a balance of power in your intimate relationships. You should be able to trust your partner(s) and be treated with respect.

~ Many 2eA people are accused of lacking empathy, when they may actually have too much. Avoidance may be an attempt to cope with an overwhelming empathic response. Help your partner understand what your withdrawal or shutdown looks like and what you need to do to recover enough to re-engage.

~ Arguments can be very difficult for 2eA people, as they may feel an intense all-or-nothing reaction to fighting. Some of the things you can do to help work through issues with your partner(s) are: develop an ability to de-escalate your reactions and regulate your emotions; work to see multiple perspectives to the action or the problem; have a sense of humor; always plan for change; acknowledge incremental growth; and take the long view toward developing a healthy relationship.

~ Know when to say when. If the relationship does not contribute to your well-being, leaves you feeling bad about yourself, or is abusive in any way, give yourself permission and take action to end the relationship.

Life Stages

◆◆◆

How do you navigate maturing and aging when you are at multiple stages at once? What if your emotional intelligence is at a different phase than your intellectual capacity? What if your work or relationships are never parallel to typical life milestones? How can you experience growth if you are stuck at a particular developmental stage? What if you just don't fit into that typical life?

Kato

Kato loves his job. He works for a nonprofit that supports indigenous people's rights and works to provide needed resources. As a bi-racial man who grew up in an impoverished neighborhood, Kato deeply understands the needs of these communities. As a 2eA man, he knows the loss of opportunity that comes from being marginalized. He has become a specialist in supporting gifted indigenous people who are unable to access resources because of their poverty. Kato often lives for months at a time with each community, learning how best to support their needs. This allows him to connect them to resources and opportunities for their children to accentuate their gifts, realize their potential, and break the cycle of poverty.

This is a cycle that Kato knows well. He was primarily raised by his Mom, who often worked two or three minimum-wage jobs to try to make ends meet. Kato's Dad died by suicide when Kato was seven, after struggling with complex post-traumatic stress disorder for many years. Kato believes that his Dad was also 2eA, but whose giftedness was never recognized or properly supported. Kato's Mom understood how her husband suffered and was determined to find a way to help Kato have a better life. She was always his biggest champion throughout his childhood and was determined to find appropriate support for him.

She fought to enroll him in an alternative public charter school that closely met his academic needs and was an active partner with his educators. His Mom also insisted that the school provide assessments and accelerated education when they determined he was gifted. Kato grew up in a blighted neighborhood that had once been a thriving community centered around a now abandoned munitions industry. It was also home to one of the best pediatric trauma research clinics in the country, purposefully located to help children most likely to have experienced hardship. For Kato's Mom and their neighbors, this was a lifesaving resource.

This clinic was founded by an African American doctor whose research focused on early identification of complex trauma in children. Kato felt that being included in that research was partly what saved him. The clinic provided free coordinated care that was based on research and focused on early interventions. Most relevant for Kato was their connections to specialists in autism and giftedness, who were able to identify and support Kato in appropriate ways. His Mom felt they truly partnered with them, and that made all the difference in her ability to access that level of care.

Having the support of this community allowed Kato to understand his needs and advocate for himself. He learned to ask for help at school when he was feeling stressed, or to talk to the doctor about his sensory overwhelm. With the support of the clinical and school teams, he was able to heal from his own trauma. He could utilize his gifts at school and was a good student. Kato graduated from high school with honors and attended college on a scholarship. His early experiences with caring mentors helped Kato to recognize his own empathic gifts and ultimately led him to becoming a social worker.

After completing his licensure, Kato got a job at the research clinic in his childhood community. He was excited to begin working with some of the people who had been there for him and happy to be back home. Kato became known for his ability to help the neediest kids and could build a bond with even the most traumatized. Kato saw his own struggles in so many of the children that were on his rounds. His visits to their homes were filled with the familiar experiences of his own childhood. He knew what these children and their parents were fighting against, and he felt he had an insider's knowledge on what they needed.

After nearly a decade of working and living in his hometown, Kato's Mom had a stroke. He moved back into his childhood apartment to help care for her, but not long after that his Mom passed away. With this loss, Kato experienced a deep grief that changed his life. He felt untethered and no longer as integrated into the community. He couldn't quite understand these feelings, as he had built many relationships over his years of work. But Kato could not recapture his past energy and commitment to his work. Eventually, he quit his job at the clinic. He sold or gave away all of his Mom's furnishings and began to pare down his own belongings. "It was a way to deal with the grief. My Mom was my only living relative, and when she died, I felt severed from everyone. Even though I had friends and co-workers I cared about, something had shifted."

Grief was a tangible presence for Kato, and he felt he needed to get away from everything he had known. He bought a camper van and began to travel the country. He spent two years traveling and working many types of odd jobs to pay for food and fuel. Some considered Kato to be destitute, as he lived in his van and traveled from community to community across the country. But Kato was taking time to process his grief and found that volunteering helped support him emotionally. Whenever he found an area he wanted to stay for a time, Kato would find a paying job and someplace to volunteer. He found many different ways to help others, from working at homeless shelters to teaching adults to read. Kato felt that meeting new people and learning new jobs would keep his mind busy and help him deal with his loss.

Through volunteering, Kato eventually met the director of the nonprofit he now works for, and after volunteering for over a year, he became a permanent employee. He found himself drawn to the communities they served and felt fulfilled by the work. He liked that he was able to continue traveling to different areas, while helping solve a variety of issues in each community. Kato enjoyed learning what each community needed and utilizing his connections with the nonprofit, and numerous local and national groups, to help them find workable solutions. For example, he has helped schoolchildren gain access to technology, found transportation for elders, and supported leaders fighting for voting rights. He encounters similar problems related to poverty and marginalization wherever he goes, but each community is also unique and has problems that stem from individual needs. Kato respects the inherent wisdom of each community and feels he has always been enriched by his experiences.

Over time, he carved out a niche in helping 2eA indigenous people, particularly children, to find support from outside organizations. Kato doesn't believe he will ever have children, so he feels like this is a way for him to help the next generation. He knows that Native American 2eA children have the potential to contribute a different perspective about what is important. He sees himself in so many of the kids he works with, recognizing how deeply empathetic they are because they have experienced loss and deprivation. He believes people who have struggled have a clearer vision of what is important.

Kato is now in his 60s but doesn't even think about retiring from his job. He has simplified his life and has more than enough to meet his needs. He enjoys living a monastic life. Since he has never cared much about owning things, he tries to leave an even smaller footprint wherever he goes. Kato believes he has more freedom in living this way. He earns more than he needs to live on, which allows him to help others with his surplus. Over the years, he has upgraded his original van to a small, bio-diesel camper van built by a friend who shares his commitment to conscientious consumption. Kato always tries to buy goods that are locally grown or hand-crafted to keep the money flowing within their communities.

Kato believes in treating others with the utmost respect and kindness. He is ethical in his dealings with people, animals, and the planet. He tries to live in a way that will not cause anyone or anything to suffer. Kato is trying to create positive change through how he lives his life. He hopes it ripples out to become something greater. He credits his early life experiences for his altruistic growth, as he believes his Mom's kindness and generosity set the tone for his own journey.

Through that journey, Kato has also learned to put his judgments of others aside and tries to find common ground with everyone he encounters. He has met people from all walks of life, many whose values are very different to his own; but he understands the common language of pain. "I know that most anger and selfishness come from a place of fear. People just don't know how to free themselves from their own self-imposed prisons. I don't want to add to their self-hatred, so I try to be kind to everyone."

Kato was fortunate to have a mother who recognized his trauma and helped him to navigate those feelings in a positive way. Despite their own poverty, Kato remembers his Mom helping others in need whenever she could. "She always reminded me how lucky we were to have our health, enough to eat, and a roof over our heads. I didn't realize what an activist my Mom was until I saw the impact she made on those around her." She validated Kato's experiences, which allowed him to overcome hardship and learn to value himself. Kato feels his Mom truly built a village for him, filled with caring neighbors, teachers, doctors, and friends.

He has tried to help others to create these community safety nets throughout his life. Kato enjoys sharing his earned wisdom with others, but also feels that every elderly person should have a young mentor to help them see the world through fresh eyes. He has friends of all ages and from many cultural backgrounds. Kato believes his life is richer than it would have been if he had lived a more conventional one. He has directed his efforts toward a global family and found joy in connecting to a greater purpose. "I am never lonely or bored and I find friends everywhere I go. I don't think you could ask for much more than that. I hope I can continue this work until the day I die."

Bernie

Alfred met Bernie at Woodstock when they were both 19 and look-ing for adventure. After the festival was over, they drove across the country to San Francisco, and fell in love along the way. Over the years, they have built a life together. Through self-discovery and community activism, they have found purpose and the freedom to be themselves, something that had never been easy for Bernie.

He always knew he was different from other people. He had a hard time communicating with others, and most of his teachers thought he was mentally disabled because he rarely did his work as assigned. Bernie was not interested in what they were teaching in school. He had already taught himself to read and do math. Bernie usually made halfhearted attempts at completing his work, and often left most of it unfinished. He hated being bored and spent a lot of his class time daydreaming. When he was around the children in his neighborhood, and on the playground at school, he was often bullied and harassed. Bernie preferred to be alone and avoided other children as much as he could. His parents were heavy drinkers who fought often, so Bernie tried to stay away from them too.

Through his growing years, Bernie suffered a lot. Few people understood or supported him, and he constantly felt he was doing something wrong, but couldn't quite understand what it was. He became more withdrawn and self-doubting in his early teens. The only person around whom Bernie felt relaxed was his uncle, Jim, who owned a music store in town. Jim was a quiet, gentle person, who always welcomed Bernie to hang out at the store after school. When Bernie was 12, Jim gave him a guitar for his birthday. He spent many afternoons listening to music and teaching himself to play. When no one was bothering him at home, Bernie would spend hours in his room learning songs, which he found to be very soothing.

When Bernie graduated from high school, Jim offered him a job helping out at the store. He learned quickly and was good with every aspect of the job except chatting with customers. Jim saw that this made Bernie very stressed. He was often unable to help the customers or adequately answer their questions. Bernie was always very apologetic afterwards, but Jim told him that everyone has some things they are good at, and some they are not, so he should just focus on what he was good at. This helped Bernie to relax and feel competent at what he could do at the store.

Bernie worked for the next year and saved his money for some future plan, even though he was not sure what he wanted to do with his life. He liked routine, but he was beginning to get bored with the sameness of his days. He was also tired of living with his parents and the tension that dynamic created. One day, while at work, he saw an ad in the newspaper for "3 days of peace and music" at the Woodstock Music and Art Fair in Wallkill, New York. Bernie thought that sounded like something he would like to attend. Jim encouraged him to take a week off and go have fun. Bernie bought a bus pass, packed his clothes and guitar, and headed to Woodstock.

As someone who loved to both listen to and play music, Bernie was enraptured by the Woodstock experience. Like many in attendance, he felt at peace, at one with the universe, and in love with everything. Bernie wanted this to be his life. When Alfred introduced himself, Bernie felt an immediate attraction, one more magical part of the weekend.

Alfred and Bernie spent all three days of the festival together, and Bernie felt that Alfred was the first person his age who seemed to genuinely like him just as he was. He didn't seem to find Bernie strange or difficult to be around. At the end of the festival, Alfred asked Bernie if he wanted to go on a road trip with him to San Francisco, and Bernie said yes. They spent a month driving across the country, sleeping in Alfred's old car and sightseeing along the way.

When they arrived in San Francisco, they stayed with a friend of Alfred's while they found work and a place of their own. Bernie experienced a feeling of belonging for the first time in his life. He proudly identified as gay, and was surrounded by other young, gay men who were also seen as outsiders by mainstream society. Within this group he didn't feel his differences mattered or were even much noticed. His friends accepted that he was more comfortable playing his guitar in the corner of the room than talking at parties. They respected his sensitivity and need for quiet times. His need for routine and order were both appreciated and indulged. Bernie was often asked to help his friends organize their lives. Overall, Alfred found his quirkiness endearing and appreciated Bernie's efforts to make him happy.

Both Bernie and Alfred became activists in the fight for gay rights, which eventually led to lifetime careers. Alfred went to work as a community organizer for the newly emerging Pride movement and Bernie helped behind the scenes writing articles for related publications. Alfred's work eventually led to a lifetime serving as an elected city official, while Bernie's writing about his community became a regular column in a local newspaper. They weathered the difficulties of the early days of fighting for recognition and equality to become one of the most well-known gay couples in the city. Yet, Bernie never grew completely comfortable with being in the social spotlight, and often left parties early, or stayed home altogether.

While Bernie was aware that he struggled more with feeling overwhelmed by everyday interactions than others, he knew he was smarter than a lot of people. He didn't realize that his experiences could be defined as a form of autism. One evening, as he was driving home, he heard a discussion about Asperger's syndrome[1] on a radio talk show. Bernie was intrigued to hear them describe the traits and behaviors of people with Asperger's syndrome, as it seemed to explain all of his quirks. Bernie began to use his skills as a writer to read everything he could find about Asperger's and write notes on his research. The more he learned, the more Bernie felt he understood the reasons for his struggles. He knew that his experiences resonated with everything he had read about autism and giftedness. Bernie began to see himself, and his experiences, through a different lens.

He began to write about his journey of discovery and self-diagnosis. Eventually, he created a series of columns about Asperger's that opened a floodgate of interest from people who read his work. Bernie became somewhat of a local Asperger's celebrity and shared his stories with anyone who asked. He often mused at how different his life might have been if he had known about Asperger's when he was a child. Bernie felt motivated to build understanding that might save children from suffering as he had. He felt this was a new area of activism for him, one that was just as satisfying and rewarding as his early gay rights work.

Over the years, Bernie and Alfred created a life they loved filled with meaningful work and satisfying achievements. They had cultivated good friends and now had a circle of close companions who they felt were their true family. Their livelihoods enabled them to indulge their love of travel and adventure, as well as create a home together that made returning a pleasure. When Alfred finally retired from politics, they planned on taking a three-month world cruise to celebrate.

One morning, as they sat drinking coffee and discussing their

---

1   A previously used diagnosis to describe those who are on the autism spectrum and also have high intellect and strong verbal skills.

trip, Alfred did not remember that they had already agreed on which cruise line they would use. Bernie didn't think too much of the memory lapse, as they were in their 70s, and both were forgetful. But it became more noticeable when they were on their cruise. Bernie found that Alfred often needed a few moments to remember the words for common items. He frequently repeated a story he had told a few hours earlier or asked Bernie to remind him about the details of plans they had made.

When they returned home from their cruise, Alfred's memory worsened. He began to occasionally miss appointments and long-standing weekly gatherings with friends; but became irritated whenever Bernie questioned or reminded him about upcoming events. Despite his denials to Bernie, Alfred found that he was having difficulty with things he had previously enjoyed, such as doing a crossword puzzle or cooking a new recipe. He knew something was not right but was afraid to face what it all might mean. Bernie continued to make regular suggestions that Alfred get a checkup, but Alfred always refused.

Over the next year, Alfred's memory issues worsened. Finally, after a frightening incident where he took an Uber to an office complex but couldn't remember why he was there or how to get home, Alfred agreed to see a doctor. Even though they both suspected bad news, it was devastating to hear that Alfred had Alzheimer's. Bernie tried to be strong for Alfred, but as he listened to the doctor tell them what they could expect to happen, he felt like his world was unraveling. Alfred had been at the center of everything that had been good in Bernie's life.

Over the next few months, Bernie and Alfred had many difficult conversations about what they would do at each step of his illness. They decided to get married, as it had recently become legal, and they felt it would make any medical decisions and interactions easier. Their city hall marriage was a bitter-sweet celebration for both of them, as it was a ceremony that marked a beginning and an ending.

After their marriage ceremony, Bernie and Alfred settled into a new routine. Bernie spent more time with Alfred, both at home and accompanying him to any appointments or events he had scheduled each week. For a while, aside from Alfred's memory lapses and needed level of supervision, their lives felt relatively normal. But they both knew that would not last, as Alfred's cognitive abilities continued to decline. Eventually, he needed to be reminded who his friends were and details about their relationship, which embarrassed Alfred and curtailed his enjoyment of socializing. Alfred had possessed an ease and calm that had always helped Bernie communicate and socialize. Bernie felt that it was horribly ironic that Alfred's communication and ability to socialize now depended on him.

As his challenges increased, Alfred withdrew from friends and spent more time at home with Bernie. Then he began to occasionally forget who Bernie was and ask about people from his childhood. Bernie found that one of the activities Alfred most enjoyed was listening to music, and they spent many afternoons reminiscing about the memories each song inspired. But Bernie was at a loss about how to help Alfred reconnect to their present life. The more altered Alfred became, the less capable Bernie felt. Bernie could commiserate with Alfred's efforts to communicate his thoughts and needs, his increasing sensitivity to changes in his routine, and how much sensory input could be overwhelming for him. It seemed that Alfred's illness was a grimmer reflection of Bernie's own dis/abilities.

One of the hardest aspects of Alfred's illness for Bernie was the feeling of unpredictability, both in how he might be each day, and the uncertainty of the progression of the illness. Bernie had always needed a certain level of predictability to be able to relax and engage fully. When he was confronted by stressful events, Bernie could usually hold it together until the problem was resolved, but then needed a day or two of downtime to recover. Alfred understood this about Bernie, and they had always structured their lives to reduce Bernie's stress. When he was struggling, Alfred had always been there to help him feel secure. Now that Bernie was facing the hardest event of his life, his most trusted ally was not able to help stabilize him anymore.

Despite his fears and struggles, Bernie was determined to care for Alfred for as long as he possibly could. He wanted to stay connected and hoped being with him every day would ensure Alfred would know who he was more often. But as Alfred became more dependent, he also began to be combative. Bernie found himself trying to help Alfred dress while fending off blows or suffering insults. He also struggled to get Alfred to eat, and mealtimes became a battleground. Trying to feed Alfred triggered all of Bernie's sensory issues, as they were often both splattered with food by the meal's end. Bernie begin to have difficulty facing each day and felt more and more burned out each evening.

Finally, Bernie contacted an in-home care service and they began to have a caregiver come to their home every day. While this helped Bernie feel less overwhelmed with the day-to-day care, he was often overcome with grief. Not being embroiled in the daily care details allowed Bernie a clearer view of how much they had lost. Alfred was not himself anymore and only had rare moments of lucidity. Bernie knew that he was truly alone, even though his beloved partner was still alive.

They endured another two years of the slow erosion of Alfred's mind and body, and Bernie became more and more depressed. When Alfred finally died, Bernie felt incapable of continuing on alone. He began to consider suicide, as he felt hopeless and nonfunctional most of the time. His friends were extremely worried and tried to find ways to re-engage Bernie in life. A close friend, Rachel, who had also recently lost her partner, convinced Bernie to go to a grief therapy group with her. Bernie found that it helped to have that expectation of attendance and accountability to Rachel. He felt that was the only thing that kept him alive the first few months after Alfred's death. Over time, Bernie began to feel less suicidal. He started to look forward to going each week and became more comfortable in sharing his feelings and accepting support.

As Bernie dealt with his grief, he began to figure out ways to restructure and reconnect to life. He knew that Alfred would have wanted him to find peace and joy, and Bernie wanted to honor Alfred's memory. When he thought about ways to bring meaning into his life, he knew he must reconnect to his passions. Bernie eventually decided to begin volunteering at a center for home-less LGBTQ youth. He found that his love of activism resurfaced through supporting young people who were experiencing preju-dice, rejection, and abuse.

He became particularly involved in working with neurodi-verse youth whose struggles with assimilation and self-loathing reminded him of his own childhood pain. He is lovingly consid-ered the grandpa of the center and has helped many young people through difficult transitions. Bernie has worked to build awareness of the specific needs of 2eA people. Those around him have a better understanding of how to accommodate the challenges, and utilize the strengths, that come with being gifted and autistic. Bernie feels useful and productive most days and has found peace in his work. Many of his own anxieties and challenges throughout his life no longer seem so daunting. He has already realized his worst fears and survived. Bernie hopes that he can continue to be helpful as he ages, but no longer fears his own impermanence.

ADVICE

Erik Erikson was noted for his theory on the psychosocial stages of human development and how each stage is necessary for healthy de-velopment (McLeod, 2018). As infants, we must feel safe and cared for to develop trust in others. When we are toddlers, we learn to be independent and develop self-control; or if we are not supported, we develop a sense of shame and doubt. Growing into school age, we learn to take initiative and direct play; but if we are unable to practice this, we can develop a strong sense of failure and guilt. When we are elementary school age, we are learning to be industrious and develop competence, or we may become self-doubting and feel inferior to others.

In puberty, we develop our self-identity and sense of control of our lives. If we are not nurtured and reinforced, we will become confused about who we really are and how we fit in with others. This is crucial for our young adult years when we will find intimate partners and develop close, positive relationships with others. For teens who were not encouraged to explore roles and discover their authentic selves, intimate relationships are more difficult, and they often feel isolated and excluded.

In our mid-adult years, we are focused more on who we are in the world, and how we can contribute to our societies and generate meaningful work. If we cannot find a path toward accomplishment, we may feel we are stagnating and unproductive. This impacts the last stages of our lives, as we are reflective about what we did and how well we did it. If we feel our lives have not been well spent, we may spend our final years feeling despair and regret.

~ When we consider these stages of human development through the lens of 2eA experience, we can see how external factors may impact successful development.

» Many 2eA children's behaviors are misunderstood and their needs unmet, so they do not develop trusting, supportive relationships with their parents. Another level of difficulty can be added for those who are LGBTQ and don't feel they can embrace their true identity.

» Levels of anxiety, sensory issues, overexcitabilities, social struggles, and language deficits can further isolate 2eA people throughout their lives. Added to these experiences, not finding meaningful work or satisfying intimate relationships can leave a large hole in a 2eA person's development. For some 2eA elders, life has been an exercise in endurance that is fraught with pain and suffering. They can't look back at a life well lived, nor can they find peace with what remains.

~ At any stage in our adult lives, we can re-examine our perceptions and change our attitudes and actions. Deepak Chopra (2007) recommends building a satisfying life through increasing our awareness and connection. We can correct negative self-narratives and be open to embracing all experiences. The more perspectives we are willing to examine, the more capable we become at building acceptance for difference. For 2eA people, it may be necessary to reject the story that others have told you about yourself throughout your life. You may need to examine your own beliefs and embrace your differences. You can practice radical self-acceptance that will free you to recalibrate your life.

~ Life is unique for each person, and we all have to learn what works for us through trial, error, and life experience. Many 2eA people have felt they don't fit in, that life is not designed for them, or that their approach to life is not valid. It takes courage and perseverance to try and fail until you find your path.

~ Many 2eA people are attuned to life in a different way than neurotypical people. They may be very empathetic from an early age and can experience existential depression when what they observe around them clashes with their empathic innocence. Young 2eA children may react strongly to what they see and hear happening around them and may be deeply wounded by the cruelty or insensitivity of others. They often try to assert activism however they can, such as refusing to eat meat or trying to raise money for a cause. Parents and caregivers should nurture this empathy and validate their 2eA children for trying to make a difference.

~ Finding meaning in your life is an essential human need. It is an important contributor to good health and longevity. According to the Blue Zone Study, having a meaningful purpose is a major con-tributor to a long life (Buettner, 2008). Belonging to a community and feeling connected are also crucial aspects, as is finding healthy outlets for releasing stress. You can create a life that will likely be long and healthy, through incorporating each of these aspects of Blue Zone living into your daily practice.

~ There are many cultures that value a good work-life balance, where time for relaxation and connection are as important as work and productivity. Investing in people and the planet carry the same im-portance as monetary investments. However, societies often over-look the value of creating, belonging, and sharing. In many countries around the world, there is no security or feeling of community. Too often people must work multiple jobs to earn enough to survive. There may not be any governmental safety nets to provide medical or elder care, or, if they exist, what is offered is not sufficient. 2eA people may be uniquely equipped to help change this paradigm through rejecting the status quo and working for change.

~ Some people may be able to rely on their families or find/build support within their immediate community. But many 2eA people have not experienced a supportive childhood environment. Their needs may have been misunderstood and their behaviors punished. Marginalized people have to work much harder to build success into their lives. Many need support to overcome trauma and re-discover their strengths and passions. Feeling capable of growth, and having a life that fosters emotional development, is crucial to living up to your potential. If you are a person who has reached that place of stability and success, see what you can do to help others within your community to do the same.

When Life Gets
Even Harder

❖❖❖

EVERYONE EXPERIENCES HARDSHIP in their lives, yet many 2eA people's hardships are caused or exacerbated by lack of understanding and acceptance. This can be especially painful when they are facing health issues, as many 2eA people have physical characteristics and responses that are not well understood by professionals. They may find that their experiences and complaints are dismissed or overlooked and they need to be activists when they feel their least capable. Building understanding for the specific needs and unique issues related to their health and physical well-being is critical to ensuring 2eA people receive the care they deserve.

Lana

Lana has lived with multiple sclerosis (MS) for almost ten years and is an activist within the MS community. Activism comes naturally to her, as she grew up knowing she is autistic and gifted, raised by parents who founded a nonprofit designed to build awareness and create opportunity for autistic children. Lana's uncle, Sean, is also autistic, but had a very different experience growing up, which is why her father vowed to find a way to help autistic people thrive.

Lana's father, Simon, grew up knowing his brother was institutionalized. Simon's parents believed that it was for the best, as Sean had behavioral problems and they were told that he would receive better support living in a residential program. Simon didn't have an opportunity to get to know his brother growing up, and Sean died when Simon was at university. Simon felt the loss greatly and vowed to find a way to help other children avoid Sean's fate.

Lana feels very fortunate to have been raised by such enlightened parents. They had a great deal of experience in supporting other autistic children and families long before she was born. They helped her to feel whole and competent, while understanding how to address her multiple challenges. Like her uncle, Lana had behavioral problems when she was young. She had outbursts when the demands and sensory input were too much for her. Emotional regulation was difficult for Lana and she was very rigid about changes in her environment. "So many of my behaviors could have led to mistreatment and subsequent trauma. I am so grateful that my parents knew what was going on and how best to help. I had an unremarkable childhood because I had remarkable parents."

Her parents found a school designed to support gifted autistic children and moved across the country so she could attend. Lana loved her school and felt it helped her to develop her strengths. She never felt disparaged for her differences, as she was with others who had similar challenges and gifts. Additionally, her teachers understood what to do when she was overwhelmed or couldn't sit still and had gentle redirection strategies to help her cope.

Lana was fairly successful at building relationships with her classmates and was content with the social interactions she had at school. While she considered her classmates her friends, Lana didn't have much desire to see them outside of school. She enjoyed time alone and could always fill her free time with interests and activities. Lana wasn't particularly focused on relationships with other people.

Then Lana discovered that she was a runner. Not only did she find it thrilling to run, but her long, lean body was perfectly designed for speed. Her school had a sports program, and students 12 years and older could try out for various teams. Lana joined the track and field team when she was 12 and became a star runner early on. Much of her self-identity and social circle developed through running. She developed close relationships with her teammates through their shared love of running. Lana enjoyed competing and her speed got better and better each year. By the time she finished high school, she was offered a cross-country scholarship to college.

Lana decided to study kinesiology, as she became very interested in how the body moves and what runners could do to optimize their performance. She continued to participate in cross-country running throughout her schooling, until she graduated with a doctoral degree in sports medicine. Lana's expertise and enthusiasm for her sport were notable, and eventually led to a position as a kinesiologist in her alma mater's athletics department.

Lana devoted herself to her career. She loved every aspect of her job, the athletic environment, and the people she worked with each day. On weekends, she helped develop a sports program through her parents' nonprofit organization that was designed to build teamwork and athletic ability. Lana helped many children become more aware of their body's capabilities and confident in their movement. She radiated good sportsmanship and her love of running was infectious. Over her nearly 30-year career at the university, and volunteering efforts, she touched the lives of many young athletes.

When she was in her 50s, Lana's parents passed away within a year of each other. Her father died from pancreatic cancer a few short months after he was diagnosed, and her mother died quietly and unexpectedly in her sleep a year later. Lana thinks her Mom willed herself to die, as her parents had always been very close.

Their deaths hit Lana hard. She deeply grieved the loss of her immediate family and felt she would never adjust to living without them. When she was particularly down, Lana felt running was the one thing she could rely on to clear her head. She loved to run the hills around her home every evening, an experience that gave her a fleeting sense of well-being.

One day, Lana began to notice a tingling in her legs after she ran. She also began to occasionally feel too tired to get out of bed. For a high-energy person who was extremely fit, this was a new feeling for Lana. She wondered if her fatigue was due to depression. When the tingling and fatigue did not improve, she made an appointment to see her doctor. He listened to her symptoms and conducted a comprehensive exam.

When he finished his exam, the doctor told Lana that he thought she had early signs of MS. He referred her to a neurologist for further testing. When the neurologist confirmed the MS diagnosis, Lana remembers feeling a sense of disbelief. "I thought, 'No way! I am healthy, this is not possible,' when I knew it was possible. It just seemed so strange to think I had a serious disease. I went through a period of denial, but then my body began to betray me even more and I had to accept the inevitable."

While she knew that MS is a progressive disease, Lana refused to give in or give up. She began to research alternative approaches to treatment and found a significant amount of information on holistic treatment protocols on websites like MShope.com. Their recommendations resonated with Lana and she began to follow a strict diet and exercise regime designed to minimize the effects of MS. "I am pretty inspired by the stories of ordinary people who have found alternate ways to cope. I don't harbor any illusions that there are 'cures' out there, but a healthy diet and lifestyle seem to be a no-brainer to me."

Lana also dropped her work to half-time and started yoga and meditation to relax and release stress. She worried that her normal level of intensity may have caused some of her neurological problems and hoped that slowing down might also help slow her disease. She switched from cross-country running to working out at the university gym, as she was concerned she might fall and injure herself on a trail somewhere and not be able to get help. Lana exercises each day to try to maintain muscle fitness, but sorely misses her solitary runs through the hills.

She has days where she feels very depressed about her diagnosis, and others where she is angry. She feels she has taken better care of her body than most people and is infuriated to have a disease that will slowly erode the physical abilities she has spent a lifetime building. Lana is also worried about who will care for her as she becomes more debilitated. "I was always focused on the bigger picture. I wanted to do things that would have an impact for lots of people; but it makes me wonder if I overlooked something critical. Sometimes I think I should have found a partner or had a child. The timing and purpose never felt right, but it would be a comfort to know I had someone to be there for me now."

In her life, Lana has had a few relationships, but none of them serious. She felt her close relationship with her parents and friends was all she wanted. In some ways, she has always been out of sync, compared with the choices of her peers. When others were discovering romance and interested in dating, she was focused on her schoolwork. Lana was absorbed with her fitness, training, and career, when friends were settling down and starting families. As peers began to focus on careers and raising children, Lana wanted to travel and enjoy an unencumbered life during her prime. "I never understood the way most people live their lives. They don't actually find time to have fun until they retire and then are too old and sick to do any of those things they dreamed of doing."

She is happy that she was raised by parents who followed their dreams and achieved their goals of making a difference in the lives of autistic children. Lana enjoyed the closeness of their family and basked in her parents' love and approval. She doesn't regret any of her life choices, but she is afraid of going through the experience of aging and illness alone. She has several close friends, and knows she could rely on them if she asked, but she doesn't want to be a burden to anyone.

Her own parents never really needed much help or care as they advanced in years. They lived independently and were able to stay in their own home until their deaths. Lana saw them often and always felt they were getting along well. The shock of her father's diagnosis and rapid decline was difficult for both Lana and her Mom. Even though the medical team offered support and connections to social services, Lana and her Mom relied mostly on each other for support. When her Mom died, Lana felt overwhelmed by the loss and unable to process her feelings.

While she had the support of friends and colleagues, Lana never felt comfortable exposing her true level of grief. She tried to be functional at work and put on a social mask when needed. Eventually, it became too difficult to try to push through the grief each day. Lana joined an online grief group, which comforted her. She felt the members, and the therapist leading the group, truly understood her pain. Their compassionate listening, and suggestions of books, meditations, and rituals, helped her process her experiences. With the help of the grief therapist and group members, Lana was able to create a new way of living that incorporated her grief; but the process was extremely taxing.

After reading *When the Body Says No* by Gabor Maté, Lana wondered if her grief impacted her physical health, as she was diagnosed with MS two years after her mother died. She finds herself looking for any explanation for her disease and hoping for a miracle cure. "Sometimes you get desperate for an explanation and start going down rabbit holes. I am still finding it hard to accept that I have this disease, and that leads me to dig for something, anything, to try." Lana is grieving for the multiple losses of family and health. Sometimes she feels she will not be able to recover her enthusiasm for living. She holds on to a little bit of hope that the progression of her MS symptoms will be slow.

"I think I took my health for granted in some ways. I just expected to be healthy and running every day well into old age. That is part of what makes this so hard, I have to face those worries long before I thought I would." Lana is now confronting the difficult task of deciding about her long-term and advanced care. She has already included "Do Not Resuscitate" information on her phone and medical bracelet but dreads the bigger decisions that she knows she must handle.

On days where she can face her reality, Lana has been researching options for support when she can no longer care for herself. On other days she feels too depressed to even think about her future. But Lana has always been a fighter and feels she will probably be able to battle her way through her depression too. "There are times when I wonder if I should just give in; but on most days, I am thinking about ways I can still live my life, so that's something hopeful."

Ashley

Being 2eA has always been challenging for Ashley. She's worked hard at managing her differences and using her gifts. As a child, Ashley struggled with written language and verbal communication. Yet, throughout her schooling, her dis/abilities went undiagnosed because she was good at covering them up. Schoolwork was hard, but Ashley had no trouble expressing her ideas, debating topics, and communicating clearly, as long as it was not in writing. She could keep up with most conversations, but some were problematic, such as lectures, fast-paced conversation, or if there was background noise.

Like many 2eA children, her intellect and abilities helped her compensate for her dis/abilities. In high school, she memorized the main points in lectures, rather than trying to write notes. She doodled and pretended to write, so her teachers wouldn't think she wasn't paying attention. Her gifts allowed her to perform adequately at school, but she always felt she was behind. And, in some classes, she was. Ashley had always done poorly in English, usually just squeaking by on her report cards. During her senior year she was not able to keep up with required essays and failed several assignments. Through extreme effort, she was able to redo the largest essay and pass the class with a C minus grade.

Ashley was not sure she wanted to go to college, as just getting through high school had worn her out. She had always liked photography, and after graduation she picked up her hobby in earnest. Ashley dug out her camera and began to spend her free time looking at life's minute details through her lens. She found looking at small details through the eye of the camera was relaxing. She also felt she could communicate some of what she noticed through the pictures she produced. Ashley was a master at connecting small details that led to understanding the bigger picture. She had always been interested in interconnecting systems, and her photography allowed others to begin to notice details that she had always seen in the natural world.

As she focused more on her photography, Ashley decided she wanted to learn how to develop film. She offered to help out at a photographer's studio in exchange for instruction and time in the darkroom. The photographer was impressed by Ashley's natural talent and encouraged her to create a portfolio. As she became more confident in her abilities she decided to apply to art school.

A year after graduating high school, Ashley got accepted to a multimedia program at a college for art and design. Ashley was worried about failing her written assignments, so made an appointment to see a counselor at the college. After talking to Ashley, the counselor suggested she get a full neuropsychological evaluation and connected her with an agency that could help her with that.

When Ashley received the results of the evaluation, she finally felt she had the whole picture of how her brain worked. Her assessments showed that, in addition to autism, she had a processing disorder that impacted her reading and language. She also found out that she was highly gifted in visual-spatial abilities and abstract thinking. With this new information, Ashley was able to help others understand both her abilities and dis/abilities and get the appropriate support. This support allowed Ashley to persevere and eventually earn her degree.

Then she began to look for a job, hoping to find something that would allow her to use her photography skills. But the dotcom bubble had just burst, and the job market was very competitive. Ashley knew she had trouble getting her point across when she was nervous, so she practiced for interviews, even memorizing scripts of what to say for various questions. But there were always questions that tripped her up and she found she just couldn't interview well enough to get hired. After a frustrating year of trying and failing at finding a job, she gave up and decided to try freelance work.

Her communication issues made this difficult too, but she was able to secure a few small freelance jobs. The back-and-forth communication with clients, and trying to ensure she understood what they wanted, created a great deal of fatigue. There was little room for error with freelance work; if she didn't meet expectations, she was not given any future work. Ashley saw that paying customers were not going to offer her the type of support or understanding she had been given at college. Things were different out in the "real world."

She gave up on making a living as a freelance photographer and got a job in a cafeteria at a hospital. Ashley had always wanted to use her talents to work in a creative field, but she was discouraged. To capitalize on her gifts, she was required to meet expectations that had nothing to do with her talents. Trying to meet those expectations was so exhausting she had little energy to be creative. She decided that photography would just have to be a hobby for now.

One afternoon, while photographing in a local park, she overheard a woman discussing her daughter's learning difficulties. The conversation caught Ashley's attention because the woman could have been describing her own school experiences. She noticed the woman was showing a book to her companion and talking about how helpful the information was for her. Ashley worked up her courage to ask the woman if she could write down the book title so she could get a copy for herself.

She found a copy of Dr. Linda Kreger Silverman's *Upside Down Brilliance: The Visual Spatial Learner*. Ashley read and reread this book, each time finding new information that validated her experience. Something that really resonated with her was the advice that visual spatial learners should capitalize on their ability to think in images and create jobs that work for them. The book inspired her to once again try to create a way to get paid for what she was good at doing.

Ashley created a series of photos that showed small natural wonders in close-up images. One featured an ant carrying a grain of sand, another the veins on a leaf, a third zoomed in on a bee's face. Her work illuminated the beauty of things people passed by every day. She asked her boss at the cafeteria if she could hang her work on the walls and make a small photography gallery for patrons to enjoy. Her boss agreed, and Ashley hung her work.

Ashley had gotten to know some police officers who often came into the cafeteria for coffee. One day they were complaining about how difficult it was to get their fieldwork photos developed properly. Ashley pointed to her photos and told them she knew how to develop photos correctly. The officer said it couldn't hurt to let her try. The first film she developed was just a dummy roll the police officer took to see how well she did. He was impressed with the clarity of the photos and began to bring her film from his fieldwork. Soon word got out that she was fast and reliable. Ashley began to develop more and more photos for police officers.

Eventually, one of them asked her if she would be interested in actually taking fieldwork photos. Ashley jumped at the chance and began to accompany police officers and take pictures for them as they examined crime scenes. Eventually, Ashley decided to quit her hospital job and take fieldwork photos full time. Her visual abilities allowed her to capture images of items in the field that no one else had noticed, which made her highly successful at photographing the scene. This job worked for her because her visual-spatial gifts were emphasized, and communication requirements were minimized.

Late one night, as she was walking home from a job, Ashley was hit by a car. She was rushed to the hospital, but during surgery she suffered an unexplained neurological event. When Ashley woke up from her surgery, she learned she had suffered a traumatic brain injury (TBI). Suddenly, she had a much more significant level of impairment. Her language, which was already impacted by her pre-accident dis/abilities, became a major impediment. In addition, she now had a mild cognitive deficit, hearing loss, and vestibular disorder that affected her balance and movement.

This "dis/ability times three" compounded her recovery and made things a lot harder. Now Ashley's dis/abilities were more obvious, she used a cane to walk, her speech was slower, and she lost her train of thought when interrupted. Before the TBI, her dis/abilities had been much less noticeable to most people. Now she was seen by everyone as a person with dis/abilities, and people often highly underestimated her intellect.

The first year after her TBI, Ashley found, was often confused and processing was extremely slow. Ashley has had a long and arduous recovery, which was extremely frustrating for her. Most therapeutic and medical professionals did not realize the depth of her intellect or creativity. Being 2eA and having a TBI created a unique brain profile. Despite her cognitive impairment, she still had high scores in visual-spatial tasks. Many of the doctors she saw did not know she was gifted, so did not understand how much her cognitive functioning had slowed. One of the neuropsychologists told her that he had never seen any results like hers. Ashley replied, "You don't understand who I was."

She felt it was crucial that her medical team realize what she had been like before the TBI, so they could accurately assess both her abilities and dis/abilities post-accident. She eventually found a neuropsychologist who understood 2eA brains and took the time to unravel her case with all of its complex and compounding aspects.

Ashley is frustrated by how many people see her impairment but not her intellect. She finds that well-meaning people often try to help, sometimes insist on helping, when she does not need or want it. Her cognitive abilities are often more than adequate for the job at hand, but, because her speech is impaired, people believe she is incapable. Compounding the problem is her difficulty in expressing herself under pressure. The more stressful the situation, the less able she is to self-advocate.

Ashley is still fighting to engage in the world and contribute her talents. She has retained her superior visual-spatial ability and is trying to return to her photography. Despite all her setbacks, she continues to work toward finding ways to embrace her abilities and support her dis/abilities. She wants other 2eA people with TBI to know that she is working on helping professionals understand her journey, so they can be better informed about traumatic brain injury and recovery for people like her.

ADVICE

~ Medical appointments can be very stressful or triggering for 2eA people. The stimuli can be overwhelming (noise, lights, examinations, being touched, questions from medical personnel). Anything you can do to give yourself comfort during the appointment will help with coping. For example, wear your most comfortable clothing, use noise-canceling earplugs, take a comfort item with you, or bring a person you trust to the appointment.

~ If you are going to the doctor to get test results for a suspected serious issue, take someone you trust along to take notes or ask to record the conversation. You will likely be too overwhelmed to absorb all the information at that time, so having notes or a recording will allow you to take in more of the information at a later time and in smaller doses.

~ If your medical practice or hospital has a social worker or autism specialist available to patients, utilize that service. They will be able to be your interface with the rest of the medical team and that can help them better understand how the appointments or treatments might impact you.

~ Many 2eA people are sensitive to medications, including anesthetic. Make sure your care team knows any prior reactions to medication, or if you feel something is off with a new medication. If you are scheduled for a procedure or surgery, discuss your worries about the anesthesia with your doctors.

~ 2eA people often have different responses to pain, such as being more sensitive, or not able to display signs of pain in neurotypical ways. Make sure your medical team knows that typical pain check-lists to measure your level of pain might not be accurate.

~ When you are in a hospital for examinations, testing, or emergency care, transitions can be abrupt and the reasons for rapid changes are not always explained to the patient. This can be very discon-certing and overwhelming to a 2eA person. The more your medical team knows about you before you enter the hospital, the more they can help if you have a panic attack, melt down, or shut down.

~ If you are hospitalized, let the nursing staff know you are 2eA and ask for things that will make you as comfortable as possible. Most nurses are highly compassionate people and will do everything they can to help you rest and recover.

~ Many professionals involved in TBI treatment of 2eA persons may assume that the patient has recovered their normal cognitive functions before they are truly recovered. This is due to a lack of awareness of the levels of intellectual capacity prior to the injury. A person may appear to have normal cognitive functioning, but their abilities could be significantly less than they were prior to the TBI. Friends, partners, and family may need to help them understand your previous intellectual abilities. It is also important to make sure the medical team knows all of your dis/abilities, as that can impact diagnosis and recovery too.

~ Medical practitioners may not have a good understanding of 2eA, so are not able to successfully integrate treatment protocols that address 2eA needs. You may need an advocate to ensure they understand all aspects of your abilities and dis/abilities prior to your illness.

~ The effect of the TBI is likely less noticeable to professionals than it is to the affected person and those close to them. Your friends, family, and partners may need to help the professionals understand who you truly are and the extent of what has been lost.

~ A serious illness is difficult for everyone, but the overwhelming sensory and anxiety experiences can cause a 2eA person to have an equally serious mental health crisis. Caregivers need to provide understanding and ask for appropriate mental health support as part of the recovery.

~ The impact of being gifted on recovery is extremely frustrating for a person with TBI. They are usually highly aware of what is going on in their mind, but often can't express it to others. Your support team may need to help you find ways to communicate your needs and concerns.

~ Resources and programs to support one's dis/abilities rarely acknowledge giftedness, or how that influences a person's overall approach to healing. It may be critical to advocate for appropriate acknowledgement and accommodations.

~ Every person responds uniquely to illness and treatment. The nature of a person's pre-existing dis/abilities can make recovery longer and potentially create changes to the individual's personality, physiology, emotions, and cognition. It is important to have people around you who know you. They will be your touchstone in helping others understand what is lost and what you would like to regain.

~ It is important to be able to advocate for your needs throughout an illness, even those that are terminal. Dr. Atul Gawande (2014) writes about listening to what the patient wants and providing the type of care that allows them to experience what is important to them until death. Make sure your loved ones know what you want and don't want as your terminal illness progresses. Having an advocate who knows your wishes can help you die the way you want to.

Wrapping It Up

———— ◆◆◆ ————

L IKE ANY EXCEPTIONAL POPULATION, 2eA people are a distinct group who share similarities in their needs and abilities, which can be a bonding and unifying experience. Yet each person within that community is also distinctly unique in their personality, worldview, capacity, and vulnerability. As a cultural group, they have much to offer the world, but only if they can be their unique selves. If they are marginalized and oppressed, their opportunities are minimalized.

As a human population, we are at the crossroads of sustainable versus unsustainable behaviors that could determine our future possibilities. When a society is biased against some of its citizens, and rejects their contributions, we all lose. The more we embrace neurodivergence, the more likely we will utilize broadly creative approaches to our problems. We need a more innovative approach to ensure we have explored solutions from diverse minds.

As we redesign our lives to be more sustainable, we need to ensure we have included diverse voices and radical ideas. If not, we run the risk of using the insular, convergent models of those who have continually held power. Our lives should be redesigned to strengthen our varying abilities and accommodate our differences. Imagine a world where schools adjust to the needs of each child from the first time they walk into a classroom. Or a commerce that values sensitivity, creativity, and compassion over capitalism. What if a 2eA person could see a doctor with confidence in their deep professional knowledge of neurodiversity? Imagine what could be accomplished if science and medicine were advanced for enriching people instead of corporations?

The more we are open to difference, the greater the possibility for positive growth. We can collaborate as unique individuals and use our combined creative energy to make the world better for everyone. We may once again begin to place a high value on the so-called "soft skills" of compassion, sensitivity, depth of thought, mindfulness, and empathy. This can build the foundation for infusing all of our lives with potential.

It is wasteful and counterproductive to use a deficit lens to minimize someone's value. We need neurodivergent people to succeed and find acceptance in every walk of life. Children should grow up with role models and stories that reflect diverse human possibility and presentation. Each person should feel they have the right and possibility to develop their true potential and be their authentic self throughout their life.

In *Divergent Mind: Thriving in a World That Wasn't Designed for You*, author Jenara Nerenberg said she needs four things for growth, acceptance, and healing: (1) finding the right career; (2) understanding her own needs; (3) effectively communicating her needs and feeling they are respected; and (4) learning about her body and responding appropriately. These don't seem like radical requests from the fringes. I think it speaks to how difficult others have made the world for neurodivergent people.

Despite a long history of oppression, I hold hope that we are making progress toward full inclusion. I can envision a world where people are free to share their ideas, be connected, feel valued, and see themselves represented in seats of power and knowledge. I have worked for most of my adult life to try to shift my corner of the world in that direction. I want my children to live in a society that honors their individuality and provides opportunity to contribute their skills and vision. I hope they will not have to struggle disproportionately or deny their dreams because they are not valued.

I think we can create a roadmap to guide us in the direction of positive change. It starts with championing 2eA children and protecting them from internalizing the message that they are broken.

Overexcitabilities

Most 2eA people have heightened sensitivities and responses to their environment, often referred to as *overexcitabilities*. These overexcitabilities can fall under five broad categories: psychomotor, sensory, imaginational, intellectual, and emotional.

- *Psychomotor overexcitability* is the physical response to environmental stimuli and may be related to issues such as insomnia, hyperactivity, pressured speech, intense need to move, extreme sports/athleticism, and impulsivity.

- *Sensory overexcitability* increases the need to chew, touch, or handle items. It can also cause an aversion to touch or, conversely, create an increased need for specific types of physical contact (like firm hugs or weighted blankets). Stimming/ self-soothing behaviors are related to this overexcitability.

- *Imaginational overexcitability* is often linked to artistry, entrepreneurial inventiveness, and the intense need to create. It can manifest through having a vivid imagination, being able to remember and give a detailed description of images, impressions, and nuanced emotional responses. It may also be linked to having heightened anxiety and intense dreams/ nightmares.

- *Intellectual overexcitability* is often experienced as an insatiable need for novel information and the desire to achieve mastery. It leads to people finding joy in analyzing difficult logical and theoretical problems and have extreme persistence in seeking answers and acquiring knowledge.

- *Emotional overexcitability* creates deep empathy and sensitivity to others' emotions and experiences. Those with this overexcitability may be introverted, as the intensity of their interactions with others can result in self-preservation through withdrawal or avoidance. They may also experience phobias, obsessions, anxiety, existential depression, and overwhelming feelings of being alone and misunderstood (Dabrowski & Piechowski, 1977).

References

American Psychiatric Association. (2013). *Diagnostic and statistical manual of mental disorders* (5th edn). Washington, DC: Author.

Aron, E. N. (1997). *The highly sensitive person: How to thrive when the world overwhelms you.* New York, NY: Harmony Books.

Buettner, D. (2008). *The Blue Zones: 9 lessons for living longer from the people who've lived the longest.* Washington, DC: National Geographic Society.

Carr, W. C. (1960). *Hansard*, HC Debate, vol. 623, col. 1440–1450 (18 May).

Chopra, D. (2007). *The seven spiritual laws of success: A pocketbook guide to fulfilling your dreams.* San Rafael, CA: Amber-Allen Publishing.

Dabrowski, K. (1964). *Positive disintegration.* London: Little, Brown.

Dabrowski, K. & Piechowski, M. M. (1977). *Theory of levels of emotional development: Vol. 1B. Multilevelness and positive disintegration.* Oceanside, NY: Dabor Science.

Danckert, J. & Eastwood, J. D. (2020). *Out of my skull: The psychology of boredom.* Cambridge, MA: Harvard University Press.

Gawande, A. (2014). *Being mortal: Medicine and what matters in the end.* New York, NY: Henry Holt.

Herman, J. (2015). *Trauma and recovery: The aftermath of violence—from domestic abuse to political terror.* New York, NY: Basic Books.

Holmes, D. M. (2020, 19 December). To the young person who doesn't identify with their disability diagnosis anymore [Blog post]. *Mad in America.* Retrieved 3 July 2021 from www.madinamerica.com/2020/12/disability-diagnosis

Kanner, L. (1943). Autistic disturbances of affective contact. *Nervous Child, 2,* 217–250.

Kapp, S. K. (2011). Navajo and autism: The beauty of harmony. *Disability & Society, 26*(5), 583–595. doi:10.1080/09687599.2011.589192

Kerns, C. M., Newschaffer, C. J., & Berkowitz, S. J. (2015). Traumatic childhood events and autism spectrum disorder. *Journal of Autism and Developmental Disorders, 45,* 3475–3486. doi:10.1007/s10803-015-2392-y

Knapp, M. L. (1978). *Social intercourse: From greeting to goodbye.* Needham Heights, MA: Allyn & Bacon.

Levine, P. A. (with Frederick, A.) (1997). *Waking the tiger. Healing trauma: The innate capacity to transform overwhelming experiences.* Berkeley, CA: North Atlantic Books.

Marland, S. P., Jr. (1972). *Education of the gifted and talented: Report to the Congress of the United States by the U.S. Commissioner of Education and background papers submitted to the U.S. Office of Education.* Government Documents Publication No. Y4.L 11/2: G36. Retrieved 12 August 2021 from www.eric.ed.gov/PDFS/ED056243.pdf

McLeod, S. A. (2018). *Erik Erikson's stages of psychosocial development.* Simply Psychology. Retrieved 12 August 2021 from www.simplypsychology.org/Erik-Erikson.html

Myhill, G. & Jekel, D. (2015, March). Neurology matters: Recognizing, understanding, and treating neurodiverse couples in therapy. *FOCUS*, NASW Massachusetts.

Parsons, L., Cordier, R., Munro, N., Joosten, A., & Speyer, R. (2017). A systematic review of pragmatic language interventions for children with autism spectrum disorder. *PLOS ONE, 12*(4), e0172242. doi:10.1371/journal.pone.0172242

Sequenzia, A. (2016). Person first language and ableism [Blog post]. *Ollibean.* Retrieved 3 July 2021 from https://ollibean.com/person-first-language-and-ableism

Washington-Harmon, T. (2020, 13 August). *Code-switching: What does it mean and why do people do it? You might be code-switching and not even know it.* Health.com. Retrieved 3 July 2021 from www.health.com/mind-body/health-diversity-inclusion/code-switching

Index

2eA 9, 219–21
  autistic and gifted 9–10,
    16–18, 22, 24–5
  characteristics of 2eA
    people 10–14
  self-advocacy 35–6

activism 34–6, 57, 64, 65, 203
  Bernie 195–6, 200
  Kato 191–2
  Lana 204
Adverse Childhood Expe-
  riences (ACEs) 186
advice 57
  advice for parents of 2eA
    children 58–9
  advice for young 2eA adults 59–60
  college 77–80
  health issues 215–18
  homekeeping 115–19
  life stages 200–3
  partnerships 182–7
  personal care 130–2
  relationships 159–64
  social life 145–7
  work life 95–100
advocacy 34–6
  medical treatment 217, 218
African Americans 27, 62
aggression 32, 48–51
  Jonathan 133–4

Alden 126–30
allergies 120, 127, 129
  food allergies 130–1
AMC Theaters 99
American Psychiatric Association 27
Anime Expo 146
Anna 72 165–72
  Dr. Ricki 169–71
  motherhood 167–9
anxiety 22, 24, 57, 70, 88,
  91, 142, 167, 177
  homekeeping 117–18
applied behavior analysis (ABA)
  therapy 29, 41, 42, 46
arguments 187
Aron, Elaine *The Highly Sensitive*
  Person: How to Thrive When
  the World Overwhelms You 166
Ashley 210–15
  TBI (traumatic brain
    injury) 214–15
  visual-spatial abilities 213–14, 215
Asperger's syndrome 196
asynchronous development 11,
  12, 13, 115, 138, 160, 184
  relationships 160, 162–3
attachment 164, 165, 170, 184, 186–7
attention deficit hyperactivity
  disorder (ADHD) 24, 76, 167
  homekeeping 116–17
Audubon Society 108

autism as pathology 28, 34–5
  treatments 28–30
autistic and gifted 9–10,
    16–18, 22, 24–5
  emotional characteristics 12–13
  intellectual characteristics 10–11
  physical characteristics 11–12
  social characteristics 13–14
Autistic Self Advocacy Network 35
Autistic Tyla 35
Autonomous Sensory Meridian
  Response (ASMR) 80
aversive punishment therapy 29
avoidance 32, 65–6, 158, 184, 187, 222
avoidant/restrictive food intake
  disorder (ARFID) 121–2

BeBe 41–8
behaviors 24–5, 27–9, 31–2, 34, 35, 41
  BeBe 42–3, 45, 48
  Jonathan 133–4
  Julian 49–51, 54–5
  Mimi 141–2
  responses to trauma 56
Berkowitz, S. J. 55
Bernie 193–200
  Bernie and Alfred 195–200
  Jim 194
  Rachel 199
Black Lives Matter 27
Blue Zone Study 203
Boles, Blake *Better Than College:
  How to Build a Successful Life
  Without a Four-Year Degree* 95
Borderline Personality Dis-
  order (BPD) 28
boredom 116, 119
Boro Autism Support Initiative for
  Success (BASIS) Program 79
Buettner, D. 203
bullying 23, 44, 45, 55, 72,
  81–2, 127, 149, 193

Carr, W. 28
characteristics of 2eA people 10–14
childhood 28–9, 30–3, 34, 41, 203

advice for parents of 2eA
  children 58–9
BeBe 41–8
Julian 48–55
Tahnee 108–10
Chopra, D. 202
clothing 130
code-switching 60
cognitive behavioral therapy
  (CBT) 121, 123, 162
college 61, 77–80, 95
  Ashley 211–12
  Jonathan 135–6
  Kenny 62–70
  Lauren 87–8
  Reuben 71–7
  Tahnee 112–13
Comiccon 146
Comiket 146
conventions 146
Crenshaw, Kimberlé "#Say-
  HerName" 67

Dabrowski, K. 25, 222
Danckert, J. 119
dating 150, 157, 160
decompression 114, 144, 176
depression 57, 88–9, 127, 210
  Bernie 199–200
  homekeeping 118
  Lana 208, 210
  seasonal affective disorder 126–7
developmental delays 22
diagnosis 17–18, 27–8
  treatments 28–30
*Diagnostic and Statistical Manual of
  Mental Disorders* (DSM) 27, 35
disengagement 52, 64, 65–6, 71, 156
dissociation 32, 51–2, 87
Dragon Con 146
dysgraphia 76

Eastwood, J. D. 119
eating problems 121–2
echolalia 28, 63
Edinboro University 79

Education, Health, and Care
    Plans (EHCPs) 20, 52
electroconvulsive therapy 29
emotional characteristics
    of 2eA people 12–13
    Bebe 42–4
emotional dysregulation 49, 134
"emotionally disturbed" 24, 32
empathy 15, 22, 25, 59, 187
    BeBe 43–5
    Mimi 142–4
employment see jobs; self-em-
    ployment; workplace
entrepreneurship 99–100
Erikson, Eric 200
Ernst and Young 99
executive function skills 66, 68, 101
    homekeeping 117

family life 165
    Anna and Geoff 168–72
    Sam and Mark and Etta 172–82
Farr, Michael 300 Best Jobs With-
    out a Four-Year Degree 95
Feinstein, Adam A History
    of Autism 29–30
flight-or-fight response
    24, 31, 32, 51–2
food 120–4
    gut problems 121
    health 129, 130–1
Ford Motor Company 99
Fresco, Jacque 128
friends 133
    Jonathan 134–8
    Kato 192–3
    Mimi 144–5
    Sam 172–3

Gamescon 146
Gauguin, Paul 63
Gawande, A. 218
gay community 195–6
genderqueer 148, 149
generalized anxiety disorder
    (GAD) 22, 24, 91
giftedness 10, 165

Alden 128–30
Ashley 211–12
BeBe 46
gifted and autistic 16–18, 22, 24–5
Jax 83–6
Julian 49, 52–4
Kenny 62
Mimi 138–9, 143–5
Reuben 73, 74–7
Ronan 102–3, 106–7
Grandin, Temple 100
Greene, Ross 32
grooming products 131
gullibility 14, 99, 150, 161
gut problems 91–2, 120–2, 124, 125

hardship 204
    Ashley 210–15
    Lana 204–10
health issues 120, 130, 204
    advice 215–18
    Alden 126–30
    Ashley 210–15
    food 130–1
    integrative care 132
    Lana 204–10
    Mahlia 120–6
    self-care 131–2
HelpX 96
Herman, J. 24
Hire Autism 99
holding therapy 29
Holmes, D. 35
homekeeping 101, 115–19
    attention deficit hyperactivity
        disorder (ADHD) 116–17
    chores 116
    Ronan 101–7
    Tahnee 108–15
homeschooling 23, 46
homework 53, 58, 71–3
hyperactivity 124–5
hypersensitivity 131
hysteria 27–8

illness 215–18
imposter syndrome 10, 34, 96–7, 142

inclusion 65, 133, 137, 220–1
independent living 101
  creating a functional home
    environment 117
  creating a restful home
    environment 115–16
  Lauren 89–90, 94
  Ronan 103–8
  Tahnee 113–15
Individuals with Disabilities
  Education Act (UK) 2005 31
insulin shock therapy 29
integrative care 132
intellectual characteristics
  of 2eA people 10–11
  Kenny 67–8
intensity 15, 25
  Lana 207–8
  Mimi 140–1, 145
International Legal Foun-
  dation, The 97
IQ testing 19
irritable bowel syndrome (IBS) 91–2

Jax 81–6
Jekel, D. 184
jobs 80, 82, 95–6
Jobs, Steve 130
Jonathan 133–8
Julian 48–55
  Jess 50–1
  Rasha 52–5

Kanner, L. 28
Kapp, S. 30
Kato 188–93
Kendi, Ibram X. How to Be
  an Antiracist 65
Kenny 62–70
Kerns, C. 55

labels 9, 15–19, 26
  2eA children 24–5, 32
Lana 204–7
  MS (multiple sclerosis) 207–10
  Sean 204–5

language 17–18, 26
  diagnostic labels 27–8
Lauren 86, 87–94
Lawrence 153–9
Lego 73
Levine, P. 55
LGBTQ 101–2, 200, 201
life stages 188, 200–3
  Bernie 193–200
  finding meaning 202–3
  Kato 188–93
  life stages and 2eA 201–2
LSD 29
Lupron 29

Mad in America
Mahlia 120–6
marginalized people 15–19,
  35–6, 69–70, 191, 203
Marland, S. 30
Maté, Gabor When the
  Body Says No 209
McLeod, S. 200
medication 25–6, 32, 42, 50–1, 216
MegaCon 146
mental health services 42,
  57, 100, 102, 217
Microsoft 99
Mimi 138–45
Miracle Mineral Solution 29
motivation 116, 118–19
motor skills 125
MShope 207
Myhill, G. 184

Native Americans 191
Navajo/Dine'é 30
Nerenberg, Jenara Divergent Mind:
  Thriving in a World That
  Wasn't Designed for You 220
neurodivergence 15–19, 25–6, 219–21
neuropsychological evaluations
  63, 91, 165–6, 211–12
Newschaffer, C. J. 55
nonverbal learning disor-
  der (NLVD) 24, 49
nutrition see food

occupational therapy 42, 125
online classes 74–5, 107
online gaming 124, 133, 140, 146
online interest groups 133, 143, 209
"oppositional defiant disorder" 24, 32, 49
organizational apps 78
Orloff, Judith *The Empath's Survival Guide* 143
overexcitabilities 25, 80, 117, 140, 143, 165, 201
 categories of excitabilities 221–2

pain management 132, 216
panic attacks 82, 166, 169, 216
parents 29, 31–2, 34
 advice for parents of 2eA children 58–9
 Bebe 41–3, 46–7
 Bernie 193–4
 Jax 82–3, 85
 Julian 48–50, 52–4
 Kato 189–90, 192
 Kenny 62–4
 Lana 204–5, 206–7, 208–9
 Lauren 87–8, 91–4
 Mimi 139–41
 Reuben 71–6
 Sam 172–3, 175
 Xena 149–50
Parsons, L. 41
partnerships 165, 182–7
 Anna 72 165–72
 Sam 172–82
"pathological demand avoidance" 32
PAXPrime 146
perfectionism 11, 12, 81, 97, 147, 162
 Kenny 62, 65
 Mimi 140–1
 Sam 173, 177–8
Perler, Seth 58
personal care 120, 130–2
 Alden 126–30
 Mahlia 120–6
physical characteristics of 2eA people 11–12
Piechowski, M. M. 222

post-traumatic stress disorder 189
pragmatic speech therapy 41
premature birth 21–2
proprioception 125
Purple Ella 35

racism 62, 64, 67
rejection 44–6
relationships 133, 134–5, 137, 148, 159–64
 arguments 187
 authenticity 184–7
 Lana 205–6, 208
 Lawrence 153–9
 partners 182–4
 sexuality 184
 starting a family 184
 staying-together strategies 184
 Xena 148–53
Reuben 71–7
Ronan 101–7
 Jane 102–4, 106–7
 Mike and Cindy 103–6
routines 12, 13, 159–60
 Anna 168–71
 Bernie 194–5, 198
 Lauren 89, 91
 Lawrence 158
 Ronan 105
 Sam 176, 179

Sam 172–82
 Etta 172, 180–2
 Jeni 177
 Jocelyne 174
 marriage 175–9, 181–2
 motherhood 177–9
 Yori 178, 179, 181
SAP Softway 99
school 20, 22–4, 31–3, 61
 Alden 127–8
 Ashley 210–11
 Bebe 43–6
 Bernie 193
 home-health options 50–1
 Jonathan 133–4
 Julian 49–55

school *cont.*
    Kato 189–90
    Lana 205–6
    Mimi 139–42
    Reuben 71–2
    Sam 172, 173
seasonal affective disorder 126–7
selective mutism 32, 51
self-advocacy 35–6, 54, 61, 89
    Ashley 215
    college 78–9
    Jonathan 136–7
    Kenny 52–3
    Mahlia 123–4, 125–6
    relationships 163
self-awareness 137, 159
self-compassion 162
self-employment 84–6,
        99–100, 144–5
    Ashley 212–14
self-harm 50
sensory issues 25, 47, 70,
        81, 98, 101, 120
    Alden 126
    Anna 166–7
    clothing 130
    creating a restful home en-
        vironment 115–16, 131
    grooming products 131
    highly sensitive persons
        (HSPs) 166, 169–70
    house cleaning 117
    Lauren 87, 89, 91
    Mahlia 122–3, 125
    Ronan 105–6
    Tahnee 110–11, 113–14
sensory-processing disorder
        (SPD) 22, 24, 91, 124–5, 165
Sequenzia, A. 18
sexuality 15, 163–4, 165, 184
    Etta and Sam 180–2
    Lawrence 157–8
    Xena 150–3
Shatkin, Laurence *300 Best Jobs
        Without a Four-Year Degree* 95
Silberman, Steve *NeuroTribes* 65

Silverman, Chloe *Under-
        standing Autism* 30
Silverman, Linda Kreger *Upside
        Down Brilliance: The Visual
        Spatial Learner* 213
sleep 80, 89, 120
social characteristics of
        2eA people 13–14
    BeBe 44–5
    Jax 81–2
    Reuben 72
    workplace 99
social group work 42
social life 133, 145–6
    Jonathan 133–8
    Lawrence 154, 156
    Mimi 138–45
    overcoming social anxi-
        ety 146–7, 161–2
    pro-social skills 135
    Xena 151–3
special education 42, 46, 49, 51
Specialisterne 99
speech therapy 41, 42
speech-to-text apps 54, 64
stimming 57, 58, 63, 68, 221
Strategic Alternative Learning
        Techniques (SALT) Center 79
stress 32, 48
    Julian 51–5
    Lauren 93–4
    stressors 19, 21, 57, 134
studying 68–70, 79–80
synesthesia 91, 92

Tahnee 108–15
tantrums 48–9, 141–2
TBI (traumatic brain in-
        jury) 214–15, 216–17
temporary work 96
terminal illness 218
The Aspie World 35
Theory of Positive Disintegration 25
transitions 77–8
    medical emergencies 216
trauma 20, 31–3, 41, 48, 55–7
    behavioral responses 56

emotional symptoms 55–6
  Julian 54–5
  physical symptoms 56
twice exceptionality 9, 16–17

U.S. Congress 30–1
university 68, 70, 78, 80, 95
  Alden 128
  Mimi 144
  Reuben 76–7
  Sam 174–5
University of Arizona 79
University of British Columbia 55

Venus Project 128
volunteering 96
  Kato 190–1

Washington-Harmon, T. 60
withdrawal 32, 52, 72, 84,
  141, 158, 222
women's mental health 27–8
Woodstock Festival 193, 194–5

workplace 81, 95–100
  Anna 167
  BeBe 47
  Jax 81–6
  Kato 190
  Lauren 87–94
  personal awareness of
    2eA traits 98–9
  researching jobs and com-
    panies 96–7, 99
  work–life balance 97, 203
  workplace discrimination 97–8
writing 64–5, 68, 71
WWOOF 96

Xena 148–53

Yo Samdy Sam 35
young adults
  advice for young 2eA adults 59–60
YouTube 35, 59, 73, 74, 131

Zoffness, Rachel 132

An Adult with an Autism Diagnosis
A Guide for the Newly Diagnosed
Gillan Drew

£10.99 | $17.95 | PB | 176PP | ISBN 978 1 78592 246 6 | eISBN 978 1 78450 530 1

Being diagnosed with autism as an adult can be disorienting and isolating; however, if you can understand the condition and how it affects perceptions, relationships, and your relationship with the world in general, a happy and successful life is attainable. Through an introduction to the autism spectrum, and how the Level 1 diagnosis is characterised, the author draws on personal experiences to provide positive advice on dealing with life, health, and relationships following an adult diagnosis.

The effect of autism on social skills is described with tips for dealing with family and personal relationships, parenting, living arrangements, and employment. Important topics include disclosure, available resources, and options for different therapeutic routes. On reading this book, you will learn a lot more about the autism spectrum at Level 1, be able to separate the facts from the myths, and gain an appreciation of the strengths of autism, and how autism can affect many aspects of everyday life. Drawing from the author's lived experience, this book is an essential guide for all newly diagnosed adults on the autism spectrum, their families and friends, and all professionals new to working with adults with ASDs.

Gillan Drew is a writer who was diagnosed with Asperger's Syndrome as an adult. He is actively engaged with local autism charities and the Dorset Mental Health Team to raise awareness and increase understanding of Asperger's Syndrome amongst health and social services. Gillan lives with his wife and daughter in Dorset.

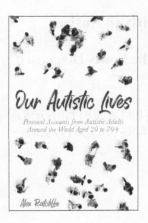

Our Autistic Lives
Personal Accounts from Autistic Adults Around the World Aged 20 to 70+
Edited by Alex Ratcliffe

£14.99 | $19.95 | PB | 272PP | ISBN 978 1 78592 560 3 | eISBN 978 1 78450 953 8

This collection of narratives from autistic adults is structured around their decades of experience of life, covering 20s, 30s, 40s, 50s, 60 and 70s+. These are varied and diverse, spanning different continents, genders, sexualities and ethnicities, yet the author highlights the common themes that unite them and skilfully draws out these threads.

Each chapter is based on accounts from one age group and includes accounts from people of that age, giving an insight into the history of autism and signifying how gaining a diagnosis (or not) has changed people's lives over time. The book is about ageing with an autistic mind, and helping the reader find connections between neurotypical and neurodiverse people by acknowledging the challenges we all face in our past, present and futures.

Alex Ratcliffe has worked within the field of autism for over 12 years. This includes working at a senior level in special educational needs and as an assessor for an autism course. She has extensive writing, researching and interviewing experience. She identifies as being autistic (self-diagnosed).

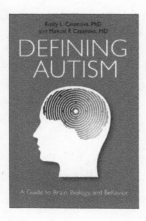

Defining Autism
A Guide to Brain, Biology, and Behavior
Emily L. Casanova and Manuel F. Casanova

£21.99 | $29.95 | PB | 264PP| ISBN 978 1 78592 722 5 | eISBN 978 1 78450 349 9

Offering a summary of the current state of knowledge in autism research, Defining Autism looks at the different genetic, neurological and environmental causes of, and contributory factors to autism. It takes a wide-ranging view of developmental and genetic factors, and considers autism's relationship with other conditions such as epilepsy.

Shedding light on the vast number of autism-related syndromes which are all too often denied adequate attention, it shows how, whilst autism refers to a single syndrome, it can be understood as many different conditions, with the common factors being biological, rather than behavioral.

Emily Casanova is a research assistant professor in Biomedical Sciences at the University of South Carolina's Greenville School of Medicine, working in close conjunction with the Greenville Health System. Her research foci include the autism spectrum and Ehlers-Danlos syndrome/hypermobility spectrum disorders.

Manuel Casanova is the director for the Childhood Center for Neurotherapeutics at University of South Carolina's Greenville School of Medicine and professor within the department of Biomedical Sciences. He is a world-renowned neuropathologist and expert on neurodevelopmental conditions.